Machine Quilting Primer

Cynthia Martin

A Quilt in a Day® Publication

To my wonderful family who has supported me every step of the way.

First printing November, 1996

Published by Quilt in a Day®, Inc.
1955 Diamond Street
San Marcos, CA 92078

1996© Cynthia Martin

ISBN 0-922705-90-9

Editor Eleanor Burns
Assistant Editor Robin Green
Art Director Merritt Voigtlander
Assistant Art Director Susan Sells

Table of Contents

Introduction

Machine Quilting is for everyone! Even if you are a beginning quilter, you can machine quilt with a little practice. As I like to say… practice makes perfect, and perfect takes practice.

I was a hand quilter until I had my second child. I then found that time was very important to me, and if I were to continue quilting it would have to be done by machine. Since making the switch, I have completed more quilts with more quilting than in all my previous years of doing the work by hand. I can complete a king size whole cloth quilt (white on white) in about a month. The quilt on the right, a king size whole cloth quilt, took me only 56 hours. Hand quilting the same quilt would have taken closer to a year. I find machine quilting is very relaxing. I hope you will find it both relaxing and enjoyable.

Cynthia Martin

How to Use this Book

This book offers six small sample practices that will help you explore various techniques of machine quilting. By going through the practices in order, you will develop the skills necessary for machine quilting. Instructions are included for a variety of fabrics and battings so that you can become acquainted with the different feels and effects they add to the look of the practices. In the beginning, I suggest that you use a spool of invisible thread on top with regular sewing machine thread in the bobbin. When you feel comfortable with your machine quilting, use some of the other suggested threads for variety. When the sample is complete, bind it with one of the methods shown in the book, then launder it so you can see the effects created when you machine quilt, and how the different battings affect the quilting.

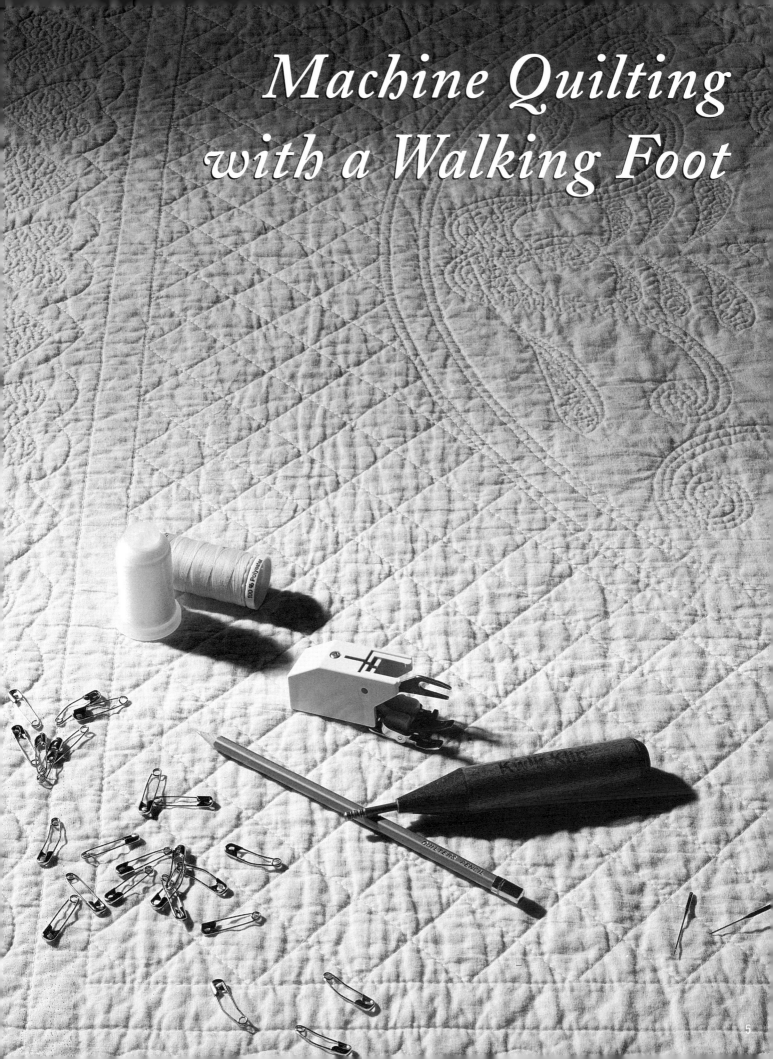

Machine Quilting
with a Walking Foot

Basics to Get You Started

Walking Foot

The walking foot, also known as the even feed foot, is an attachment that has teeth similar to those found on the feed dogs. When you have several layers of fabric to sew, these teeth help to propel the fabric layers at the same pace which helps to eliminate puckers on the front and back of the quilt. If you have ever tried to machine quilt without a walking foot, you have probably experienced puckering on either the front, the back, or both sides of the quilt.

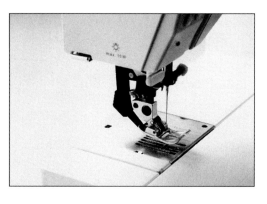

Some machines have a built-in walking foot. Having a built-in walking foot reduces the amount of set-up time in putting on a walking foot. You simply push down on the built-in walking foot to engage it and sew.

If your machine does not have a walking foot, purchase one from your local sewing machine dealer. Make sure that your dealer tests the foot on your machine and shows you how to attach it. Some dealers will sell you a generic version of the walking foot. Make sure that it fits properly, otherwise it may not function on your machine.

If your walking foot attachment isn't working, make sure that its arm is above the needle bar knob. If it still doesn't work, check to see that it is attached correctly to the presser foot bar.

Use the walking foot for straight line stitching methods such as:

- **stitch in the ditch**
- **grids**
- **outline stitching**
- **gradual curves**

Sewing Machine Thread

Use regular sewing machine thread in the bobbin. When you choose a thread for machine quilting, feel the thread. If it feels nubby or rough, it will break easily in the machine. Thread that is good for machine quilting should feel smooth without any imperfections.

When you feel comfortable with the quality of your machine quilting, use regular sewing machine thread on both the top and bobbin. Do not use hand quilting thread in the sewing machine as it is too heavy.

Invisible Thread

As you machine quilt for the first time, your stitch length and accuracy in following the design will not be perfect. Invisible thread helps hide some of the imperfections. Another advantage to using invisible thread is that you don't need to change thread color as you stitch over various colored fabrics. Choose either smoky-colored invisible thread for dark fabrics or clear for a range of colors from white to dark.

Use invisible thread in the needle and regular sewing machine thread in the bobbin case. Invisible thread in the bobbin case may explode the plastic style bobbin or ruin your bobbin case. You may need to reduce the upper tension on your sewing machine to make a balanced stitch. See page 77 for an explanation of tension adjustment.

Purchase a good quality invisible thread. Invisible thread should break easily and be about the same strength as regular thread. Look for invisible thread on a small cone. Invisible thread on a spool is generally too heavy for machine quilting and feels like fishing line. If the invisible thread is stronger than the threads in the fabric, the fabric will weaken and small holes will begin to appear around the stitch holes.

Treadle Art makes an invisible thread called Wonder Thread© that is perfect for machine quilting. If you are unable to find invisible thread on a cone at your local fabric store, try a quilt store, your local sewing machine dealer, or a quilting supply catalog.

As a word of caution, invisible thread does get old. Prior to threading your machine, check the invisible thread. If you haven't used it for awhile, it may have become brittle or yellowed. If it is yellowed, you should purchase new and throw away the old. To check its resiliency, break off a piece. If it stretches before breaking, it is fine. If it breaks instead of stretching, throw it away and purchase new.

Thread Stand

As you machine quilt, the thread should feed smoothly. If the thread loops or pulls as you quilt, you may want to try a thread stand. The thread stand sits on the table and has an extension rod which you pull the thread through prior to threading your machine. The distance between the thread guides of your machine and the thread stand allows time for knots and loops to straighten before reaching the machine. The thread stand is particularly helpful when quilting with invisible thread or with large spools of thread.

Needles

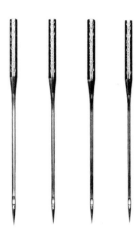

Sewing machine needle sizes increase with the size of the shaft which directly affects the size of hole made in the quilt. The larger the needle size, the larger the hole made in the quilt or fabric. For example, a size 90/14 will make a larger hole than a 80/12.

I prefer to use a Universal size 80/12 Schmetz® sewing machine needle. A 90/14 makes too large of a hole in the fabric. A size 70/10 is hard for beginners to use as the thread may break due to too much tension on the needle. Schmetz® also has a 75/11 size machine quilting needle that I use when the needle hole shows. The head of the machine quilting needle is slightly more slender than a regular sewing machine needle.

Quilter's Pencil

The Quilter's Pencil is an excellent tool for marking. It comes in a variety of colors such as blue, yellow, white, silver and pink which will accommodate almost any fabric color. Silver is my personal favorite. When the machine quilting is complete and the binding is finished, you can either leave the marks or wash the quilt to get rid of them.

The Quilter's Pencil can be sharpened either with a hand sharpener or an electric sharpener. If you are using a hand sharpener, make sure that it is the appropriate size for the pencil, otherwise the lead will break as you sharpen it.

The tip of the pencil should be kept relatively sharp. The duller the pencil, the wider the lines become. If the lead keeps breaking, it may mean that the lead is old and has become brittle. Try storing your pencils in the freezer to keep them fresh.

Quilting Guide

Some machines come with a quilt guide which is attached to the walking foot. The tool allows you to guide the quilt along existing lines of the quilt block at an even spacing without having to draw all of the lines. Some guides are better than others. The guide which comes with the Elna 9006 has a long bar which actually rests on the fabric for about 3". This allows you to sew straight along the line. Be careful not to turn the fabric as you sew, as this will cause the sewn line to be not straight.

Hera Marker

The Hera Marker is a plastic tool with a sharp edge that is used to press in the lines to be sewn. It is held in much the same way as a rotary cutter with a ruler. Line up the marker with the ruler and push the tool away from you. The marker creases the fabric as you push, leaving a non-permanent line.

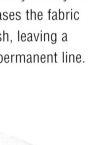

Safety Pins

Nickel-plated safety pins in the 1" size are best for machine quilting. They are small enough to prevent the layers from moving as you machine quilt, and they are rust resistant. Pins will rust if left in a quilt for several months, especially in a humid climate. Brass pins, although pretty, bend too easily to be effective.

The Collins company manufactures curved safety pins. The curve makes inserting the pin through fabric layers much easier. Curved pins are also easier to close than the straight variety.

Safety pinning takes the place of hand basting layers together. You cannot baste with thread for machine quilting because as you sew, you may sew through the basting threads, making them very difficult to remove.

Quilter's ¼" Tape

Quilter's ¼" tape is similar to masking tape. It is generally used to gauge ¼" seams but it can also be used as a straight line guide. Place it along the line to be sewn and use it as a guide instead of drawing lines.

Quilter's Straight Pins

Quilter's straight pins have a long shank and a small ball on the end for you to grasp. Quilter's straight pins can be used for basting small projects. When using them for basting, make sure that all layers are included in the pinning.

Although straight pins are not practical for pinning an entire quilt, they can be used for stitch in the ditch on the border. Insert them so that they cross the border at a 90 degree angle.

Another use for straight pins is to fix a pucker or hump when sewing. For a pucker, remove the stitches at least ½" on either side of the pucker. Insert one or more straight pins to smooth out the area and re-sew. When you notice a hump occurring in front of the walking foot, insert one or more straight pins to smooth the area and continue to sew.

When using straight pins, remove the pins just prior to sewing across them so that you don't damage the needle.

Kwik Klip™

Kwik Klip™ is a tool used to open and close safety pins. The Kwik Klip™ fits into the hand and has a ribbed tip that catches the safety pin for easy closure. After the safety pin has been inserted into the quilt layers, use the tool to guide the safety pin closed. It can also be used to open closed safety pins.

Clips

Quilt clips are open rings, designed to hold a rolled quilt. There are several different types. All will hold the quilt rolls neatly.

Bicycle clips are less expensive but bend easily and tend to slide on the quilt roll.

Jaws™ are made of a plastic and are durable. They also have teeth so they slide less on the quilt.

Quilt Clips™ can be used to hold layers taut to your working surface when pin basting as well as to hold the rolled quilt. Because of the plastic construction, these clips will not snag the fabric.

Stiletto

This tool has a point on one end and a handle on the other. It is generally used to help feed fabric under the sewing foot. For machine quilting, it is used to pull the bobbin thread up to the surface when beginning and ending sewing, and for removing stitches.

Quilter's Soap

Quilter's soap, found at most quilt shops, has an Orvus base. There are several on the market for washing quilts and comforters. Orvus is soap made for washing animal hair and is especially gentle for quilts. Bulk Orvus can be found at animal supply stores. A little Orvus goes a long way. You may need only two tablespoons of Orvus to wash a full size quilt.

Get Comfortable

A comfortable position is very important to the success of your machine quilting. You must be able to relax. Free motion quilting is almost impossible when your shoulders are tense. The more relaxed you are, the easier your machine quilting will become. You will find that your stitches will be straighter and more even. You'll need a comfortable chair that can be adjusted for height. If your chair does not adjust, sit on a pillow or phone book to raise your position so your arms make a 90 degree angle to the sewing surface.

Light

You need good light for machine quilting. I have a halogen lamp that I place next to my sewing table just for machine quilting. Halogen lighting is the closest to outdoor light and the easiest to see by.

A good overhead light or spots can also be assets. Overhead light will increase the visibility of the quilt surface and allow you to see the lines drawn on your quilt.

Two sewing space circuits—one 20-amp circuit for the iron and a separate 15-amp circuit for the rest of your equipment and accessories are suggested. The outlet for the iron could easily be placed where you are most likely to work and at a height which will provide maximum use of the cord's length.

Sewing Surface

In order to quilt, you must have space to the left, front and back of the machine. Avoid anything such as cabinet knobs which would catch on the quilt as you sew. On the back and left hand sides, you need at least three feet in order to support the quilt. If your sewing table is not large enough, you can place card tables or ironing boards on the left and back of the sewing table to create additional space. If the quilt isn't supported, it will pull and be difficult to move when quilting.

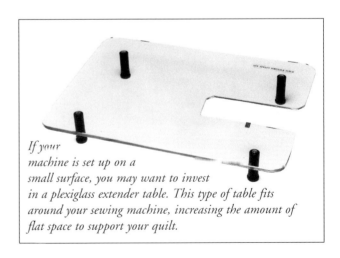

If your machine is set up on a small surface, you may want to invest in a plexiglass extender table. This type of table fits around your sewing machine, increasing the amount of flat space to support your quilt.

You can make super sewing tables from a kitchen type table, customizing the table so the machine is flush with the surface. A black rectangle of plexiglass insert manufactured by Parsons can be purchased to custom fit around your machine.

Custom order a plexiglass insert to fit your sewing machine.

Cut out a rectangle of wood 10½" x 19⅛", from the table which is the same measurement as the black plexiglass insert. Cut a 9½" x 23" platform from ½" plywood to attach under the cutout on blocks cut the height of the sewing machine base. Once the sewing machine is set on the platform, the plexiglass insert fits around the machine and makes a flat surface great for machine quilting. Blank inserts can also be purchased to fill in the hole when the table is used for other purposes.

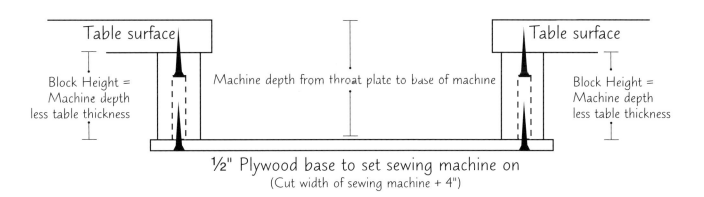

Table surface

Block Height = Machine depth less table thickness

Machine depth from throat plate to base of machine

Table surface

Block Height = Machine depth less table thickness

½" Plywood base to set sewing machine on
(Cut width of sewing machine + 4")

Practice One

Stitch in the Ditch and Grid Quilting

The following pages describe the various types of machine quilting techniques using a walking foot.

Stitch in the Ditch

Stitch in the ditch, using a walking foot, is simply straight line machine quilting in the seam where two pieces are joined. Set the stitch length for stitch in the ditch between 3 and 4 mm or 8 to 10 stitches per inch.

Stitch in the ditch when you machine quilt borders, lattice, and Quilt in a Day® quilts such as:

- **Log Cabin**
- **Tulip Quilt**
- **Applique in a Day**
- **Winning Hand**
- **Sunbonnet Sue**
- **Pioneer Sampler**
- **Flying Geese**

Tulip Quilt

Grid Quilting

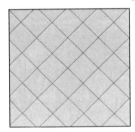

Grid quilting is stitching on evenly spaced lines drawn horizontally, vertically, or diagonally. Draw the grid on the quilt top with a marking pencil at an even spacing prior to making the quilt sandwich. You can even machine quilt all three types of grids on the same quilt alternating the grid styles in the open areas of the blocks.

Use grid quilting to create interest in the open areas of quilts such as:

- **Stars Across America**
- **Applique in a Day**
- **Bits & Pieces**

Stars Across America

Materials for Straight Line and Grid Quilting

Materials:

two 18" squares quilter's muslin
one 18" square 3 oz polyester batting
two 3" wide strips for binding

 Silver marking pencil

 3" Cellophane tape

 75 one inch Safety pins

 Jaws™

 Kwik Klip™

 Quilter's straight pins

 Walking foot

 Stiletto

 Thread for the bobbin

 6" x 24" ruler

 Invisible thread

 Rotary cutter

Muslin

Use good quality muslin in all quilting projects. Muslin comes in many different grades from cheese cloth to quilter's muslin, the best type for quilting. The better the grade is the tighter the weave.

Batting

Use thin polyester batting, 3 ounce weight, for this practice because it's small. A thinner batting will allow it to be manipulated easily and will lay flatter. For more about batting, see pages 72 and 73.

Marking One Layer of Muslin

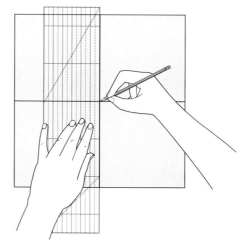

1. Divide one 18" square of muslin into four quarters by drawing lines at the halfway point both horizontally and vertically.

2. Draw lines diagonally in the first square spaced 1½" apart. Draw the first line diagonally across the square. Line up the ruler's 1½" measurement line on the drawn line to draw the next line.

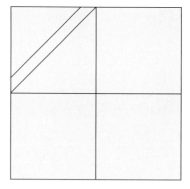

3. Draw lines vertically in the second square spaced 1½" apart.

4. Draw lines horizontally and vertically 1½" apart in the third square.

5. Draw lines diagonally 1½" apart in both directions in the fourth square.

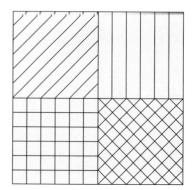

Making the Quilt Sandwich

1. Place the other 18" square of muslin on a table as if it were quilt backing. Smooth the fabric without stretching and secure it to the table with tape.

2. Place the batting on top of the backing.

3. Place the marked muslin piece on top of the batting, face up.

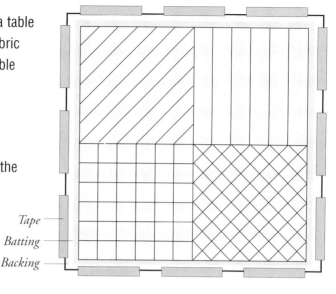

Tape

Batting

Backing

Pinning the Layers

1. Grasp the opened pin in your writing hand. Push the pin through the three layers, touching the pinning surface to ensure that you have pinned all the way through. Bring the tip of the pin back up to the top.

2. Insert the safety pins 3 to 4 inches apart, being careful not to pin where you will quilt.

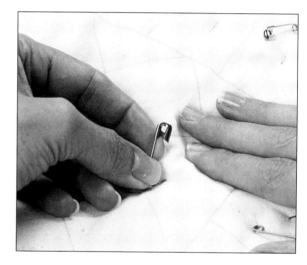

Closing the Safety pins

1. Hold the Kwik Klip™ with your writing hand. Grasp the safety pin with your other hand. The head of the safety pin should rest along your first finger with your thumb pressing down on the end of the safety pin.

2. Catch the tip of the safety pin in the groove of the Kwik Klip™ and allow the point of the safety pin to extend far enough to push pin closed.

3. With the tip of the Kwik Klip™, lift the safety pin and press down with your finger to close the pin. This process may take a few tries to get the hang of it.

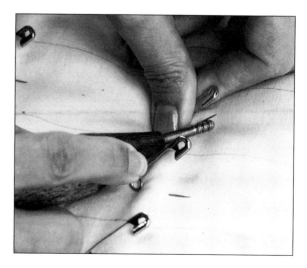

4. Close the safety pins as you go, or if you prefer, insert all the pins and then close them.

Setting Up Your Machine

1. Thread the machine with the invisible thread. Lessen the top tension. Thread the bobbin with regular sewing thread.

2. Engage your walking foot and set the stitch length to 3 to 4 mm or 8 to 10 stitches per inch.

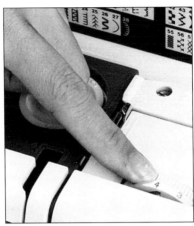
Normal Tension

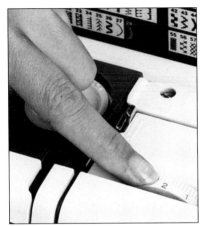
Lowered Tension

Securing the Quilt

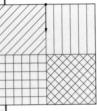

1. Roll the sample vertically toward the center and secure with Jaws™ to practice using clips. Slip the quilt under the walking foot at the spot marked in the illustration.

2. Place your hands on either side of the vertical line. Make a triangular shape with your fingers slightly spread. This gives the same effect as an embroidery hoop. Using your hands, spread the quilt flat. Feel for lumps and folds underneath the quilt. Smooth the backing and adjust your hand placement.

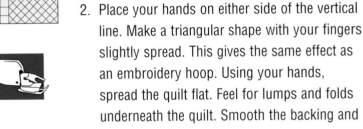

3. Backstitch at the beginning. Sew on the vertical line and backstitch at the end. Clip loose threads as you go.

4. Rotate the sample one quarter turn and re-roll toward the center and secure with Jaws™. Sew the remaining vertical line. The two vertical lines that you have sewn will secure the layers of the quilt so they won't slip.

Bringing the Bobbin Thread to the Top at the Beginning

Bringing the bobbin thread to the top of the quilt keeps the threads from being sewn in.

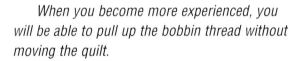

1. Roll the quilt diagonally toward the lines drawn in the first square and secure with Jaws™.

2. Insert the needle at the spot marked in the illustration.

3. Raise the needle and move the quilt 1" to 2" away from the needle.

   When you become more experienced, you will be able to pull up the bobbin thread without moving the quilt.

4. Grasp the top thread with your fingers and pull gently. You should see a loop coming from the bobbin. Pull the bobbin thread to the top.

5. Re-insert the needle in the same hole. Pull up any slack in the bobbin thread by grasping and pulling gently on the top and bobbin threads.

Machine Quilting Diagonals

1. Backstitch by sewing several stitches close together. This can be done by shortening your stitch length.

2. Sew diagonally to where the sewing line was previously sewn and backstitch.

   If your machine allows, you can also stitch in the same spot, one stitch on top of another, and then sew forward.

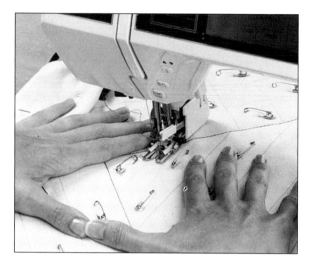

Bringing the Bobbin Thread to the Top at the End

1. Raise the needle and move the quilt 1" to 2" away from the needle.

2. Grasp the top thread with your fingers and pull gently. You should see a loop coming from the bobbin. Stick a stiletto or a quilter's straight pin through the loop and pull the bobbin thread to the top. Clip the loose threads.

3. Sew remaining diagonals.

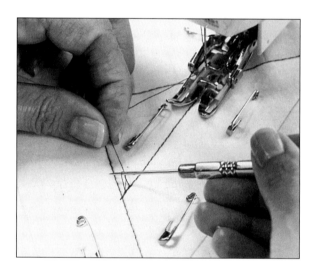

Built-in Locking Stitch

Some of the new top of the line machines have a built-in locking stitch. When you begin to sew, the machine will take several small stitches in place which locks the stitches, and then continue to sew. You may not be able to pull up the bobbin thread with the locking stitch. Clip threads on the top and underneath.

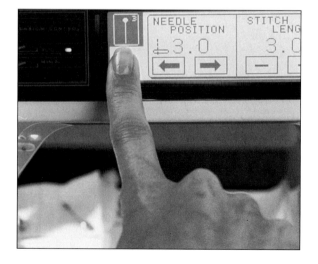

Preventing Puckers and Humps

Puckers are folds that have been sewn across on the top or the back of the quilt. A hump is a small amount of excess fabric that gradually forms in front of the walking foot. If a hump is not flattened prior to crossing a previously sewn area, it will create a pucker. By following a few simple steps, you can eliminate them.

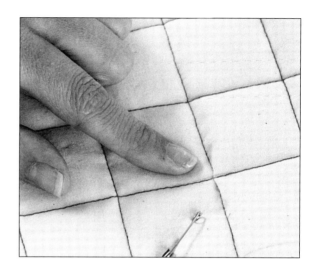

1. If you consistently get puckers or humps, your backing may have been too loose, or you may have needed to pin closer.

2. Make sure that your hands are placed in a triangular shape with your fingers slightly spread. Using your hands, spread the quilt flat.

3. Feel for puckers. If you feel any lumps, reach your hand under the quilt and smooth it. Then adjust your hand placement.

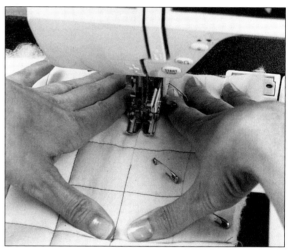

4. If you are sewing a grid or over a previously sewn line, spread your fingers vertically to stretch the fabric apart. This helps to avoid puckers or humps that occur at intersections.

Unsewing Puckers

If you get a pucker, un-sew using either of these two methods:

Unsewing Puckers with a Stiletto or Seam Ripper

1. Using a stiletto or seam ripper, break a thread loop approximately ½" on either side of the pucker.

2. Pull out the thread between and clip it away on both sides of the quilt.

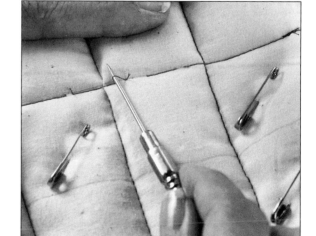

3. Re-sew, making sure that you spread your fingers vertically to stretch the fabric as you sew.

4. If necessary, add one or more straight pins to flatten and ease the hump of fabric.

Unsewing Puckers with a Rotary Cutter

1. Using a seam ripper, clip a loop of thread approximately ½" on one side of the pucker. Pull up a few stitches towards the pucker with a seam ripper.

2. Grasp the thread pulled up, and touch the loops with your rotary cutter as you pull on the thread. Be careful to cut only the thread loops and not the quilt.

3. Re-sew, making sure that you spread the fabric.

Machine Quilting Verticals

1. Roll the quilt vertically toward the lines drawn in the second square and secure with Jaws™. Insert the needle at the spot marked in the illustration and bring the bobbin thread to the top.

2. Check for lumps. Backstitch. After you sew a few stitches from the beginning, clip threads. Sew vertical line starting at the center, locking stitches at the end. Pull up bobbin thread and clip.

3. Sew remaining verticals.

Machine Quilting Horizontals and Verticals

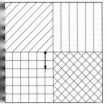

1. Roll the quilt vertically toward the lines drawn in the third square and secure with Jaws™. Insert the needle at the spot marked in the illustration. Bring the bobbin thread to the top.

2. Check for lumps. Backstitch. Sew on vertical line, locking stitches at the end. Bring up the bobbin threads and clip.

3. Sew remaining verticals.

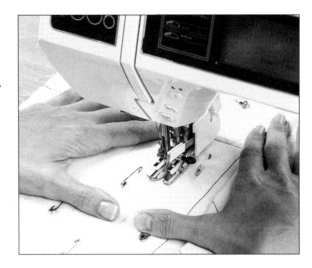

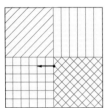

4. Re-roll the quilt vertically toward the remaining lines and secure with Jaws™. Insert the needle at the spot marked in the illustration, and bring the bobbin thread to the top.

5. Check for lumps. As you come to lines already sewn, spread your fingers vertically to avoid puckers that occur at intersections.

6. Backstitch. Bring up bobbin threads and clip.

7. Sew remaining lines.

Machine Quilting Diagonals in Two Directions

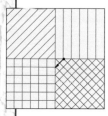

1. Roll the quilt diagonally toward the lines drawn in the fourth square and secure with Jaws™. Lower foot, insert the needle at the spot marked in the illustration. Bring the bobbin thread to the top.

2. Check for lumps. Backstitch. Sew vertical lines starting at the center, locking stitches at the end. Bring up bobbin thread and clip.

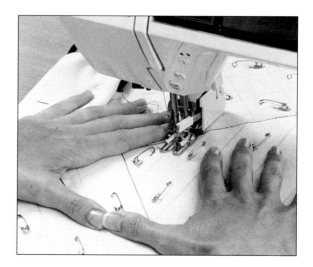

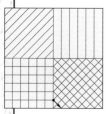

3. Re-roll the quilt vertically toward the remaining lines drawn and secure with Jaws™. Insert the needle at the spot marked in the illustration. Bring the bobbin thread to the top at the beginning.

4. Check for lumps. As you stitch up to lines already sewn, spread your fingers vertically to stretch the fabrics apart and help avoid puckers.

5. Backstitch. Bring up bobbin thread, and clip.

6. Sew remaining lines.

Binding

Binding is the finishing touch to a quilt and should be practiced. Two different bindings are included in this book. By practicing different bindings, you will decide which method you like better.

1. Right sides together, sew short ends on 3" wide strips.

2. Follow traditional binding method on page 82.

Removing Safety Pins

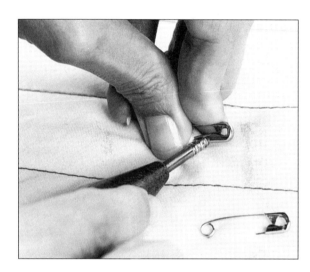

1. Hold the Kwik Klip™ with your writing hand. Grasp the closed pin in your other hand.

2. Catch the tip of the safety pin in the groove of the Kwik Klip™ and allow the point of the safety pin to extend far enough to push pin open.

3. With the tip of the Kwik Klip™, lift the safety pin and press down with your finger to open the pin. Open and remove all safety pins.

4. Do not close the safety pins. Keeping them open will eliminate the time needed to open them later. Store the pins in a plastic container with a cover such as a butter tub.

Launder (Optional)

Laundering removes any oils that rubbed off from your hands and pencil marks. After laundering, the quilt will have a softened, puckered, antique look.

1. Half fill the washing machine with tepid, not hot, water. Add quilt soap to the water. Follow directions on package, or add approximately two tablespoons per washload.

2. Agitate to disperse soap and add finished quilt to water. Use gentle agitation to wash.

3. Once the wash is complete, put into the dryer and dry with low heat, not hot. Remove promptly.

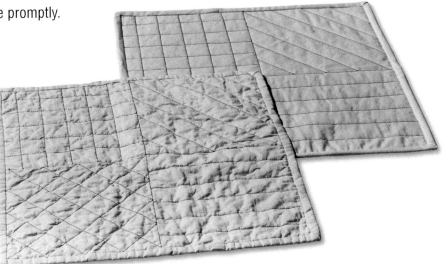

Practice Two

Stitch in the Chain and Continuous Curve

The following pages describe the various types of machine quilting techniques using a walking foot.

Stitch in the Chain

Stitch in the chain is machine quilting sewn diagonally through the chain using a walking foot. This can be done by either marking the lines directly on the quilt with a marking pencil, a Hera Marker, or ¼" quilter's tape, or simply by eyeballing the points. Set the stitch length between three and four mm or 8 to 10 stitches per inch.

Use this technique to stitch in the chain in Quilt in a Day® quilts such as:

- **Irish Chain**
- **Snowball**
- **Bits & Pieces**
- **Christmas Traditions**
- **Burgoyne Surrounded**
- **Trip Around the World**
- **Morning Star**

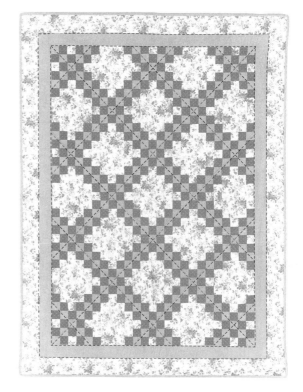

Irish Chain

Continuous Curve

Continuous curve quilting with the walking foot is sewing a gradual curve from corner to corner of squares in the chain. You do not need to mark continuous curve.

Use the continuous curve technique for Quilt in a Day® quilts such as:

- **Trip Around the World**
- **Irish Chain**
- **Bits & Pieces**
- **Snowball**
- **Christmas Traditions**
- **Morning Star**

Trip Around the World

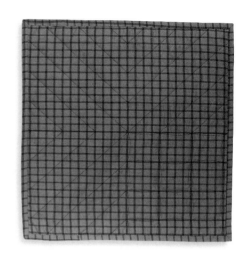

Stitch in the Chain and Continuous Curve

Materials:

one 18" square 3 ounce polyester batting
one 18" square even plaid fabric such as gingham
one 18" square quilter's muslin, backing
two 3" wide strips for binding

 Contrasting marking pencil

 3" Cellophane tape

 75 one inch Safety pins

 6" x 24" ruler

 Kwik Klip™

 Hera marker

 Walking foot

 Quilter's guide

 Thread for the bobbin

 Stiletto

 Invisible thread

 Quilter's tape

Plaid Fabric

For this project, use a piece of even plaid for the quilt top. The word "even" means the plaid will be the same size across the entire piece of fabric, both horizontally and vertically. Look for a plaid that has approximately 1" obvious squares.

Dividing the Plaid into Sections

1. Divide the fabric into four quarters by drawing lines with the pencil at the halfway point both horizontally and vertically.

2. A variety of techniques and tools may be used to mark the quilting lines.
   Square 1. Hera Marker
   Square 2. ¼" Quilter's Tape
   Square 3. Quilter's Guide
   Square 4. Hera Marker and continuous curve sewing

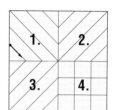

3. In square three, place the 6" x 24" ruler diagonally across the center of the 9" square through the corners of the plaid. Draw one pencil line. You will be using the Quilter's guide in this square.

Making the Quilt Sandwich

1. Place the backing fabric on a table face down. Smooth the fabric without stretching and secure it to the table with tape.

2. Place the batting on top of the backing. Place the plaid fabric on top of the batting, face up.

Marking Squares One and Four with the Hera Marker

1. In Square One, place the 6" x 24" ruler diagonally across the center of the 9" square through the corners of the plaid.

2. Hold the Hera Marker in your writing hand. Hold the ruler with your other hand.

3. Place the Hera Marker along the ruler at the edge of the square and push it away from you. Push hard enough to make a crease in the fabric. The technique is similar to that of a rotary cutter with a ruler. Repeat the marks approximately 1½" apart to fill Square One.

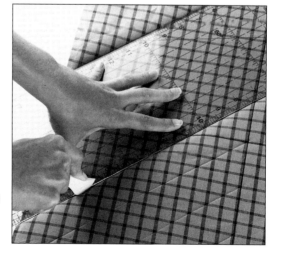

4. In Square Four, place the 6" x 24" ruler vertically across the square, approximately 1½" from the center line, through the corners of the plaid. Repeat the marks to fill the square, then turn, and mark in the opposite direction.

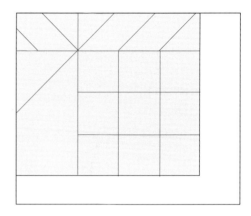

Setting Up Your Practice

1. Pin the quilt sandwich together.

2. Thread the machine with the invisible thread. Lower the top tension. Thread the bobbin with regular sewing thread.

3. Engage your walking foot and set the stitch length to 3 to 4 mm or 8 to 10 stitches per inch.

4. Secure the layers by stitching the vertical and horizontal lines.

Sewing Square One and Four with Hera Markings

1. Roll the quilt diagonally toward the lines drawn with the Hera Marker. Insert the needle at the spot marked in the illustration. Bring up the bobbin thread.

2. Place hands in a triangle, and backstitch. Sew, following the line drawn with the Hera Marker. Backstitch, bring up the bobbin thread, and clip.

3. Sew remaining diagonals along Hera lines.

Marking and Sewing Square Two with ¼" Tape

1. Un-roll approximately twelve inches of tape. Place the end of the tape to the left side of the center of the 9" square. Lay the tape diagonally across the square, from corner to corner on the plaid. Make sure the tape is stuck down.

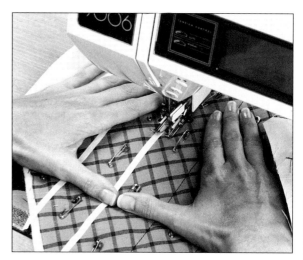

2. Repeat the tape marks approximately 1½" apart to fill Square Two.

3. Roll the quilt diagonally toward the taped lines made with the ¼" tape. Insert the needle at the spot marked in the illustration. Bring up the bobbin thread.

4. Place hands in a triangle, and backstitch. Sew, following the line made with tape. Backstitch, bring up the bobbin thread, and clip.

5. Sew remaining diagonals along tape.

Sewing Square Three with Quilter's Guide

1. Roll the quilt diagonally toward the line. Insert the needle at the spot marked in the illustration. Bring up the bobbin thread.

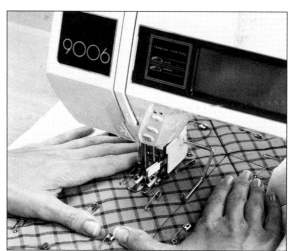

2. Place hands in a triangle, and backstitch. Sew, following the line. Backstitch, bring up the bobbin threads, and clip.

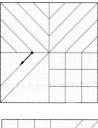

3. Insert the quilter's guide. Adjust the guide by sliding it in or out to a distance approximately 1½" that follows the line previously sewn. Insert the needle and bring up the bobbin thread. Pull up any slack. Backstitch.

4. Sew remaining diagonals on that side using the guide. Watch the location of the guide instead of the foot. Try to keep the guide on the sewn line.

5. Once you have completed that side, turn the fabric around and sew the remaining diagonals with the guide.

Sewing Square Four with Continuous Curve

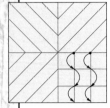

1. Roll the quilt vertically toward the fourth square. Insert the needle at the spot marked in the illustration. Bring up the bobbin thread.

2. Place hands in a triangle, and backstitch. Sew, gradually curving away from the Hera marked square. At the center of the square, your sewn line should be approximately ⅛" to ¼" from the vertical line. Once you reach the center gradually curve back toward the corner of the next Hera marked square.

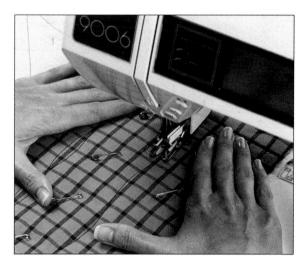

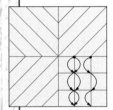

3. Continue through the center of the intersection, and curve in the opposite direction in the next square. Repeat until you reach the edge alternating curves from side to side. Backstitch, bring up the bobbin thread, and clip.

4. Starting back at the top, sew the continuous curve on the opposite sides from those previously sewn. Repeat for remaining lines drawn with the Hera marker.

Finish The Practice

1. Bind, using reverse traditional binding method on page 84.

2. Remove safety pins and launder.

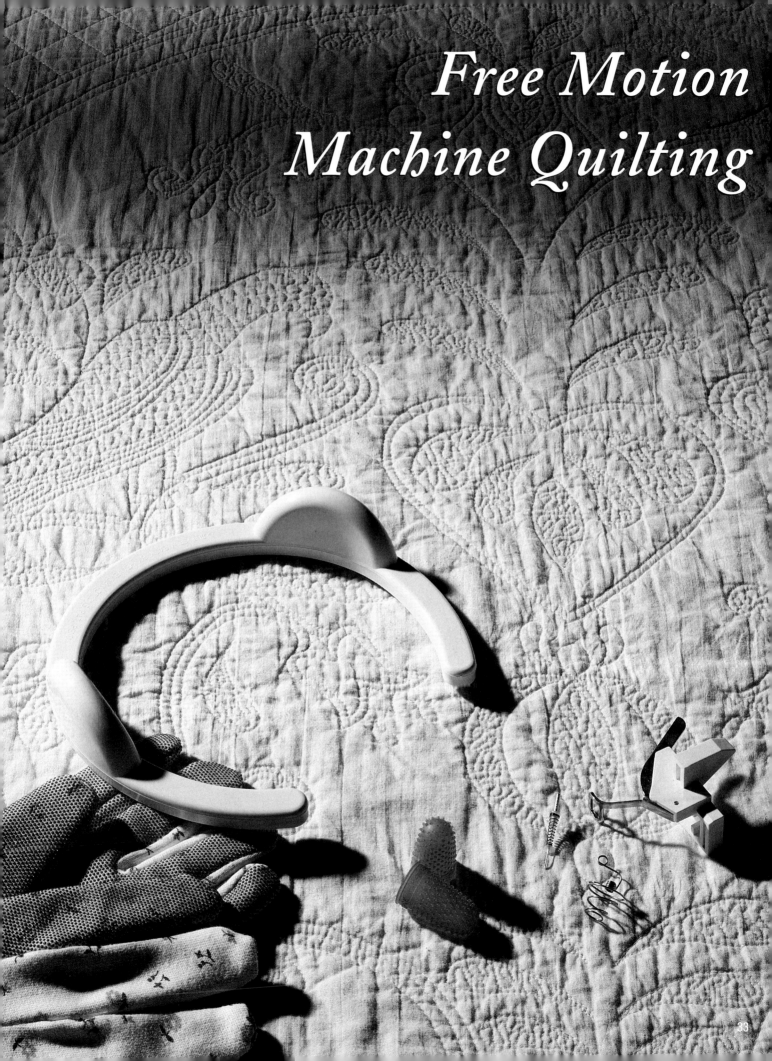

Free Motion Machine Quilting

Basics to Get You Started

Darning Foot or Embroidery Foot

The darning foot is an excellent tool for free motion machine quilting. Although its regular use is darning, this attachment allows free movement of the fabric when the feed dogs are dropped. When the needle bar descends, the fabric is held by the darning foot for a stitch and released, allowing the fabric to move. You are in complete control over how long or how short your stitch length is.

Feed Dogs

When you use the darning foot, either drop or cover your feed dogs. Each machine is a little different, so look in your sewing machine manual for information on dropping or covering the feed dogs.

Some feed dogs are covered by a snap on metal plate. If you have trouble moving the quilt when the feed dogs are covered, try taping a business card with a needle hole in it over the feed dogs.

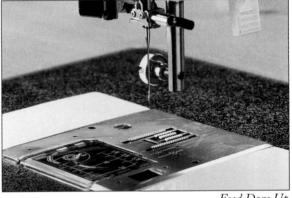

Feed Dogs Up

Feed Dogs Down

If your machine does not have a darning foot or you cannot acquire one, two inexpensive alternatives are the darning spring or the spring needle.

Darning Spring

The darning spring fits over the needle and is held in place by bending the spring's arm across the needle bar knob. You must be careful each time you use the darning spring. If you bend it in the wrong place you may need to remove, straighten, and reposition. The thread goes around the spring and through the needle. The darning spring fits all machines and is inexpensive.

Spring Needle

This is a special needle with a spring attached to it. If you move the quilt too quickly, the needle often breaks. You can replace the needle about 5 times or until the plastic part that holds the spring and needle together stretches. Once it stretches you will need to replace the whole spring needle.

Stencils

Quilt stencils are patterns cut into mylar, a heavy duty plastic film available in a variety of weights. When you choose a stencil, start out with an easy pattern. The best beginner stencils allow continuous motion, starting and ending at the same point. If you are not sure whether a stencil is continuous or not, trace it with your finger. If you can start and end at the same point without backtracking, it is a continuous motion stencil.

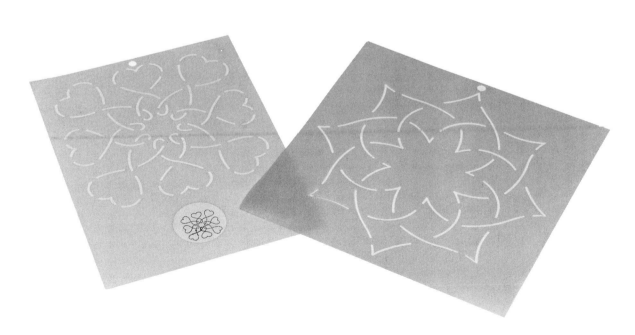

Use one of these next items to help grip and move the quilt.

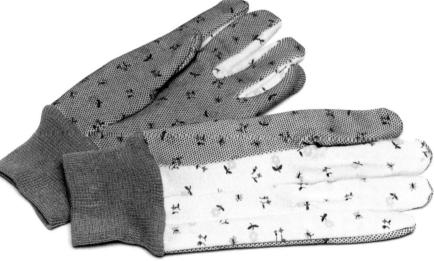

Quilt Sew Easy™

The Quilt Sew Easy™ is a flexible plastic semi-circle, used to hold and move the quilt as you are free motion quilting. Simply rest your hands on the handles and move the quilt with the tool. Move it around on the quilt top as you are quilting simply by lifting it and changing its position. Quilt Sew Easy™ flattens your quilt top for you. For those of you with arthritis, this tool is a must. Dropping your shoulders to hold the tool as you quilt makes it easier for you to relax.

Garden Gloves

Garden gloves provide another way to get a grip on your quilt. They have little bumps on them that add traction to your hands. Make sure you get a pair that fit well. If they are loose they won't add the needed traction, and if they are tight they will be uncomfortable.

Rubber Finger Tips

Rubber finger tips have nubs on them which add traction to your fingers to help you move the quilt as you sew. They come in several different sizes, so you may want to try them on before you purchase them.

Practice Three

Stitch in the Ditch with a Darning Foot

Stitch in the ditch is machine quilting in the seam where two pieces are joined. Using a darning foot is helpful when you have a lot of internal areas to stitch or if the stitch in the ditch is not in a straight line. Quilting free motion with the darning foot eliminates the need to turn the quilt in different directions. Use this technique to stitch in the ditch in Quilt in a Day® quilts such as:

- **Dresden Plate**
- **Star Log Cabin**
- **Winning Hand**
- **Courthouse Steps**

Continuous Curve with a Darning Foot

Continuous curve is machine quilting in a gradual curve between the corners of a square. The darning foot can be used for sewing continuous curve when turning the quilt is difficult. Use the continuous curve technique for Quilt in a Day® quilts such as:

- **Trip Around the World**
- **Irish Chain**
- **Bits & Pieces**
- **Snowball**
- **Christmas Traditions**
- **Morning Star**

The following pages describe the various types of machine quilting techniques using a darning foot.

Winning Hand

Single Irish Chain

Stitch in the Ditch and Continuous Curve

Cheater's Cloth

Materials:

    one 18" square Warm and Natural® cotton batting

    one 18" square cheater's cloth

    one 18" square quilter's muslin

    two 3" strips of contrasting fabric or cheater's cloth
        for binding

 75 one inch Safety pins

 3" Cellophane tape

 Darning foot, darning spring or spring needle

 Garden gloves

 Kwik Klip™

 Rubber finger tips

 Quilt Sew Easy™

 Quilter's tape

 Thread for the bobbin

 Invisible thread

Cheater's Cloth

Cheater's cloth is a term used for a piece of fabric with a design printed on it. Some examples are pre-stamped pillow fabrics, pre-stamped vests, and pre-stamped small quilts. Select a fabric that has a definite pattern printed on it, then free motion machine quilt the piece.

Batting

Warm and Natural is a bonded cotton batting. It is denser than polyester, and because it is bonded, it can be quilted up to 10" apart.

Setting Up Your Practice

1. Make your quilt sandwich and pin the layers together, using the techniques from the first two sample practices.

2. Thread the machine with invisible thread. Lower the top tension. Thread the bobbin with regular sewing thread.

3. Remove or disengage the walking foot and put on the darning foot, darning spring, or spring needle. Drop or cover your feed dogs.

Hand Placement Method

Use the triangular placement of your hands to hold and move the quilt. When you drop your feed dogs, your hands are the only control over the movement of the quilt. If you remove your hands or stop moving, the sewing machine will stitch in the same spot until you move again.

1. Slip the quilt under the darning foot along the printed line of the motif.

2. Place your hands to either side of the printed line. Put on garden gloves or rubber finger tips to help grip and move the quilt.

3. Make a triangular shape with your hands. Spread your fingers slightly. This will give the same effect as an embroidery hoop.

4. Using your hands, spread the quilt flat. Feel for lumps and check for folds underneath. If you feel a lump, reach your hand under the quilt and smooth it.

5. Readjust your hand placement. If you have pinned well you should be able to quilt at this point.

Stitch in the Ditch with a Darning Foot

If there are obvious lines on your cheater cloth, you can stitch in the ditch with a darning foot.

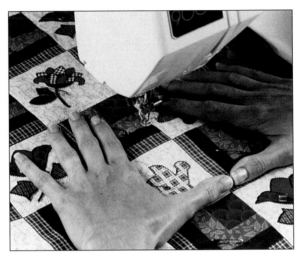

1. Insert needle at the starting point.

2. Raise the needle and bring the bobbin thread to the surface.

3. Reinsert the needle into the same hole. Sew two stitches forward and two stitches back. Clip loose threads.

4. Follow the line of the design. Lock stitches and bring bobbin thread to the top. Clip loose threads.

Stay on the Line

You will need to practice staying on the line. Always keep the design oriented in the same position. Sew left or right, up or down, but always with the same orientation.

1. Keep your eye on the needle. Don't look at the darning foot. At the same time, you must watch the line of the motif.

2. If your lines are too light to be seen easily, darken them.

Control Stitch Length

Stitch length is controlled by how fast or how slowly you move the quilt under the needle and by the speed of the machine. Controlling these two factors will take some practice. Stitches should look evenly spaced. If you loose control of your stitch length, the long and short stitches will give the quilted line an irregular appearance.

1. Try moving the quilt at an even pace. Use moderate speed.

2. If this doesn't work, try speeding up the machine but keeping the same even pace. Some students feel they have more control when the machine is moving a little faster.

Continuous Curve with a Darning Foot

If there are obvious squares in your cheater cloth, try the continuous curve method with a darning foot.

1. Insert needle at the starting point.

2. Raise the needle and bring the bobbin thread to the surface.

3. Reinsert the needle into the same hole. Sew two stitches forward and two stitches back. Clip loose threads.

4. Gradually sew a curve away from the edge of the square so that the curve is ⅛" to a ¼" away from the line at the center of the square. Gradually curve back until you reach the next corner. Continue through the intersection of the square, curving in the opposite direction. Repeat until you reach the edge, alternating the curve from side to side. Backstitch, bring up the bobbin thread, and clip threads.

5. Repeat on the opposite side of each square.

Free Motion Quilting Around a Motif

The first time you try free motion machine quilting you may feel a little out of control. The key is to relax and to practice.

1. Insert the needle at any point along the edge of the motif.

2. Raise the needle and bring the bobbin thread to the surface. Pull up the slack in the thread.

3. Reinsert the needle into the same hole. Sew two stitches forward, and two stitches back. Clip loose threads.

4. Continue to follow the line of the motif. When you reach the point where you started, lock the stitches as before. Bring the bobbin thread up to the top and clip loose threads.

Finish The Practice

1. Bind, using the traditional binding method on page 82.

2. Remove safety pins and launder.

Practice Four

Stippling and Clamshell

The following pages describe the various types of machine quilting techniques using a darning foot.

Stippling

Stippling is random stitching on background areas. A favorite method for beginning machine quilters, stippling adds a lot of dimension to the quilt and is very easy to do. Stippling tends to flatten out the quilted section, highlighting the area it surrounds. The highlighted area likewise appears to puff up. Lines are not marked to keep the pattern random. There are three major types of stippling which are quilted free motion with the darning foot:

- **regular stippling**
- **line stippling**
- **loops**

Regular Stippling

Regular stippling curves back and forth and from side to side to make tight curves that do not cross. The objective is to avoid crossing stitches. The size of the stippling depends upon the area to be stippled. In small areas or small quilts, I like stipple lines very close together. On larger quilts I expand the stippling, machine quilting further apart. Sometimes you lose the motif design if your stippling is too close together.

Line Stippling

Line stippling zigs and zags in straight lines creating points as you go. Be careful not to cross stitches. This technique is very interesting in contemporary quilts.

Loops

Loops are machine quilted in a looping motion. In this technique, the stitches cross. Use these stippling techniques with such Quilt in a Day® quilts as:

- **Stars Across America**
- **Flying Geese**
- **Ohio Star**
- **Bears Paw**

Clamshell

Clamshell is a free motion quilting technique in which small regular curves are quilted in a continuous line. The rows of the clamshell pattern alternate to create the effect. Several rows of clamshell quilting help draw attention to blank or background areas. Although the clamshell pattern can be quilted free motion without lines it will look more precise if you mark the area prior to quilting it. Use a coin or spool base as a template to draw your lines.

Stippling and Clamshell

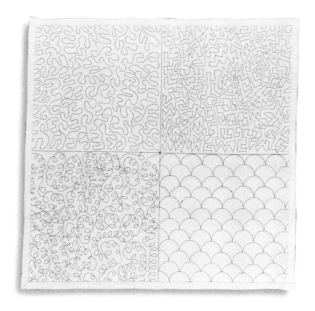

Materials:

two 18" squares quilter's muslin
one 18" square Heirloom® cotton batting
two 3" wide strips for binding
optional pillow form

 75 one inch Safety pins

 Marking pencil

 Darning foot, darning spring or spring needle

 3" Cellophane tape

 Kwik Klip™

 Walking foot

 Quilt Sew Easy™

 Invisible thread

 Thread for the bobbin

 6" x 24" ruler

Batting

Hobbs Heirloom cotton batting drapes well and is very easy to sew.

Marking One Layer of Muslin

1. Divide one piece of muslin into four quarters by drawing lines at the halfway point both horizontally and vertically.

2. Leave three of the four squares blank. In the fourth square, draw clamshell.

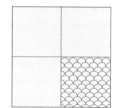

Drawing Clamshell

1. Use a spool as a template. Make a mark evenly dividing the spool from side to side and from top to bottom.

2. Place the spool in the fourth square next to the vertical and horizontal line. Rotate spool until one line on the spool is horizontal.

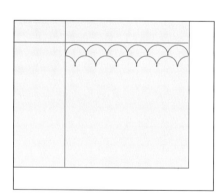

3. Draw half the spool shape. Keeping the spool horizontal, move it to the end of the previous arc drawn.

4. Draw another half spool shape. Repeat across. The template may not be even at the side of the quilt.

5. Move the spool back to the vertical line. Center the spool on the line, matching the two marks made on the spool. Draw ¼ spool shape.

6. Keeping the spool horizontal, move it to the end of the previous arc drawn. Draw another half spool shape.

7. Repeat across. The template may not be even at the side of the quilt. Alternate spool shapes to fill the space.

Setting Up Your Practice

1. Make the quilt sandwich and pin. Secure the layers, using techniques from previous practices.

2. Remove or disengage the walking foot. Put on the darning foot, darning spring, or spring needle.

3. Drop or cover your feed dogs.

Hand Placement with the Quilt Sew Easy™

1. Slip the quilt under the darning foot in the first unmarked square.

2. Place the Quilt Sew Easy™ so that it surrounds the first square with the darning foot in the center.

3. Grasp the handles of the Quilt Sew Easy™ and spread the tool outward slightly. This gives the same effect as an embroidery hoop.

4. Check for lumps.

Sewing Square One with Regular Stippling

1. Insert the needle at the corner where the squares meet.

2. Raise the needle, and bring the bobbin thread to the surface. Pull up the slack in the thread. Lock the stitches.

3. Sew a few stitches in one direction, then curve around and back toward the beginning making a loop. Remove safety pins as you sew.

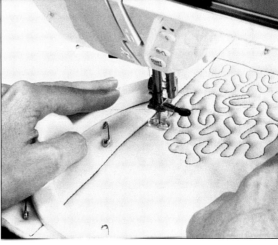

4. Before you reach the point where you began, curve back toward where you started without crossing previously sewn stippling. Continue making loops until you fill the corner. Move toward the edge and lock the stitches. Clip loose threads.

Sewing Square Two with Line Stippling

1. Slip the quilt under the darning foot in the second unmarked square.

2. Place your hands on both sides of Square Two or use the Quilt Sew Easy™. Check for lumps or folds.

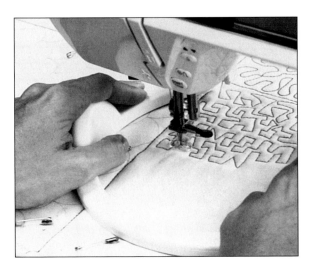

3. Insert the needle at the corner where the squares meet.

4. Raise the needle and bring the bobbin thread to the surface. Pull up the slack in the thread. Lock the stitches.

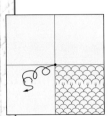

5. Sew a few stitches in a direction then sew a few stitches at approximately 30 degrees toward the beginning making a V-shape. Remove safety pins as you sew.

6. Before you reach the point where you began, sew a few stitches at approximately 30 degrees towards where you started the initial V-shape. Continue to make V-shapes until you fill the corner. Move towards the edge and lock the stitches. Clip loose threads.

Sewing Square Three with Loop Stippling

1. Slip the quilt under the darning foot in the third unmarked square.

2. Place your hands on both sides of Square Three or use the Quilt Sew Easy™. Check for lumps or folds.

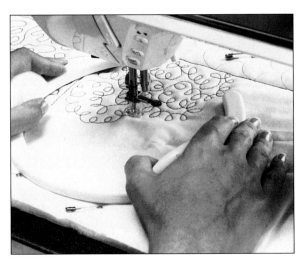

3. Insert the needle at the corner where the squares meet. Raise the needle, and bring the bobbin thread to the surface. Pull up the slack in the thread. Lock the stitches.

4. Sew a few stitches in a direction, then curve around and back toward the beginning, making a crossed loop. Remove safety pins as you sew.

5. Before you reach the point where you began, curve back toward the beginning of the initial curve, crossing previously sewn stippling. Continue to make loops until you fill the corner. Move toward the edge and lock the stitches. Clip loose threads.

Sewing Square Four with Clamshell

1. Slip the quilt under the darning foot in the fourth marked square.

2. Place your hands on both sides of Square Four or use the Quilt Sew Easy™. Check for lumps or folds.

3. Insert the needle at the corner where the first line of arcs drawn with the spool meets the vertical line.

4. Raise the needle and bring the bobbin thread to the surface. Pull up the slack in the thread. Lock the stitches.

5. Sew, following the first line of arcs. Remove safety pins as you sew. Lock the stitches. Clip loose threads.

6. Insert the needle at the corner where the second line of arcs drawn with the spool meets the vertical line. Raise the needle and bring the bobbin thread to the surface. Pull up the slack in the thread. Lock the stitches.

7. Sew, following the second line of arcs. Lock the stitches. Clip loose threads.

8. Continue sewing the remaining clamshells.

Finish the Practice

1. Bind, using the reverse traditional method on page 84 or optional pillow directions on page 62.

2. Remove pins and launder.

Practice Five

Motif, Echo and Outline Quilting

The following pages describe the various types of machine quilting techniques using a darning foot.

Motif Quilting

Motif quilting is machine quilting following the curved lines drawn on your quilt top with a stencil. Use a darning foot to quilt these lines. Quilts with background squares or triangles are especially suitable for motif quilting.

Try this technique with Quilt in a Day® quilts such as:

- **Tulip Quilt**
- **Snowball**
- **Dutch Windmills**
- **Irish Chain**
- **Bits & Pieces**

Outline Quilting

Outline quilting is sewing at a specific distance away from and around a motif, block, or square. Use the edge of your darning foot as a guide to maintain an equal distance from the motif. A little bit of deviation is all right but the more accurate the distance is the better it will look.

Use outline quilting when you want the design of the quilt block to stand out. Stitch one line about ⅛" to ¼" away from the design. Outline quilting requires a steady hand.

Use this technique to free motion quilt the outline in the following Quilt in a Day® quilts:

- **Applique in a Day**
- **Dutch Windmills**
- **Sunbonnet Sue**

Echo Quilting

Echo quilting is sewing several lines at a specific distance away from and around a motif, block, or square. Echo quilting creates a ripple effect. Free motion machine quilt with the darning foot about ⅛" to ¼" away from the original motif. Continue quilting lines approximately the same distance apart to fill in the area.

Use this technique in such Quilt in a Day® quilts as:

- **Applique in a Day**
- **Dutch Windmills**
- **Sunbonnet Sue**

Motif, Echo, and Outline Quilting

Materials:

    one 18" square Wool Naturally™ batting
    two 18" squares quilter's muslin
    two 3" wide strips for binding
    optional pillow form

 Silver marking pencil

 Darning foot, darning spring, or spring needle

 Hera marker

 Quilt Sew Easy™, garden gloves, or rubber finger tips

 Hearts stencil (provided in back of book)

 Thread for the bobbin

 75 one inch Safety pins

 Invisible thread

 Kwik Klip™

 3" Cellophane tape

 Walking foot

 6" x 24" ruler

Batting

Wool Naturally batting is light and easy to work with. Wool batting is warmer than cotton, and rolls tighter than the cotton or polyester battings, making it easier to quilt.

Marking One Layer of Muslin

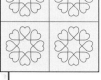

1. Divide one piece of muslin into four quarters by drawing lines at the halfway point both horizontally and vertically.

2. Remove the heart shape stencil from the back of the book.

3. Center the stencil on each square. With the silver pencil, lightly trace in the lines on the stencil, so you can see them without straining your eyes.

4. Make the quilt sandwich, pin the layers, and close the safety pins.

Setting Up the Practice

1. Thread the machine with invisible thread. Loosen the top tension. Thread the bobbin with regular sewing thread.

2. Engage your walking foot and set the stitch length to 3 to 4 mm or 8 to 10 stitches per inch.

3. Secure the layers by sewing on the horizontal and vertical lines.

Setting Up Your Machine for Free Motion Quilting

1. Remove or disengage the walking foot.

2. Put on the darning foot, darning spring, or spring needle.

3. Drop or cover your feed dogs.

Motif Quilting the Four Squares

Use your hands with garden gloves or finger tips or the Quilt Sew Easy™ to hold the quilt. Repeat the following in all four squares.

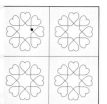

1. Insert the needle on the right side and near the tip of one of the hearts.

2. Raise the needle and bring the bobbin thread to the surface. Pull up the slack in the thread. Lock the stitches, and clip threads.

3. Sew, following the line of the motif. Control stitch length, as outlined in the previous sample practice.

4. Sew around each heart continuously. Do not turn sample practice as you sew. When you quilt a large quilt, you will not turn it as you sew. When you reach the point where you started, lock the stitches as before. Bring the bobbin thread up to the top and clip loose threads.

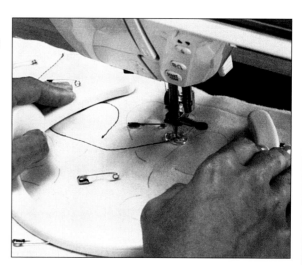

By the time you complete the third or fourth square you should be feeling a little more confident. When your stitches look nice and fairly even, go on to the next steps. If your stitches still look uneven or you aren't happy with the appearance, mark another sample practice and try again until you feel comfortable with the motif quilting technique.

Outline Quilting Squares One and Four

1. Slip the quilt under the darning foot.

2. Place your hands to either side of the stitched motif or use the Quilt Sew Easy™. Check for lumps.

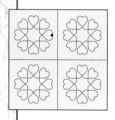

3. Insert needle ⅛" to ¼" from the outside edge of the motif. Lock the stitches.

4. Sew around the outside edge of the motif ⅛" to ¼" until you reach the starting point. Lock stitches.

5. Outline stitch inside center. Lock stitches.

6. Outline stitch around the motif in square four.

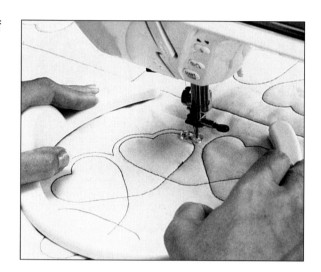

Echo Quilting Square Two

1. Slip the quilt under the darning foot.

2. Place your hands to either side of the sewn motif or use the Quilt Sew Easy™. Check for lumps.

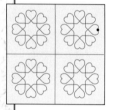

3. Insert needle ⅛" to ¼" from the outside edge of the motif. Lock the stitches.

4. Sew around the outside edge of the motif ⅛" to ¼" until you reach the starting point. Lock stitches.

5. Insert needle ⅛" to ¼" from the previous outline or echo, staggering the starting point. Lock stitches.

6. Repeat echo two to three more times until you fill the space.

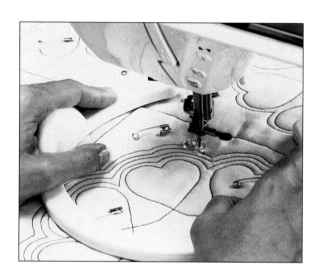

Stippling Square Three

In this square, practice one of the stippling techniques you learned in the previous section.

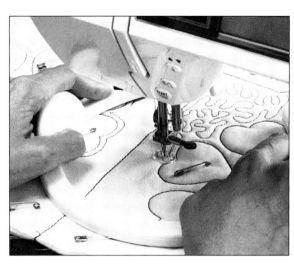

1. Slip the quilt under the darning foot.

2. Place your hands to either side of the sewn motif or use the Quilt Sew Easy™. Check for lumps or folds.

3. Insert the needle on the motif line previously sewn. Bring the bobbin thread to the surface. Pull up the slack in the thread. Lock the stitches.

4. Stipple around the motif with your favorite of the three stippling techniques. Be careful not to box yourself into a corner. Remove safety pins as you sew.

5. When you have filled the square around the motif, move towards the edge of either the motif or the securing lines sewn and lock the stitches. Clip loose threads.

Marking Square Four with a Hera Marker

1. Place the 6" x 24" ruler diagonally across the center of the fourth square.

2. Hold the Hera Marker in your writing hand. Hold the ruler with your other hand.

3. Place the Hera Marker along the ruler at the edge of the square and push it away from you. Push hard enough to make a crease in the fabric.

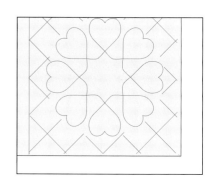

4. Repeat the marks approximately 1½" apart to fill the square around the motif. Turn the square and repeat marking to make a grid around the motif.

Diagonal Grid Quilting Square Four

In this square, practice the grid techniques you learned in previous sections.

1. Remove the darning foot.

2. Raise feed dogs or remove the feed dog cover and engage your walking foot. Set the stitch length to 3 to 4 mm or 8 to 10 stitches per inch.

3. Slip the quilt under the walking foot. Place your hands to either side of the sewn motif or use the Quilt Sew Easy™. Check for lumps or folds.

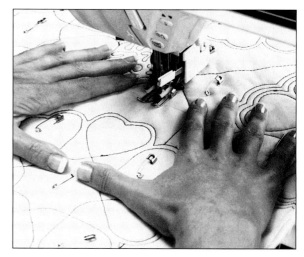

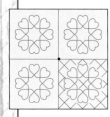

4. Insert the needle on the horizontal line previously sewn. Raise the needle and bring the bobbin thread to the surface. Pull up the slack in the thread. Lock the stitches.

5. Sew along diagonal line drawn until you reach the motif. Backstitch. Clip loose threads. Jump across the motif. Lock stitches. Continue to the edge.

6. Continue to sew diagonals, jumping over motif each time.

7. Fill the square around the motif in both directions diagonally, locking stitches and clipping loose threads.

Finish the Practice

1. Bind, using the reverse traditional method on page 84 or optional pillow directions on page 62.

2. Remove pins and launder.

Practice Six

Feathers

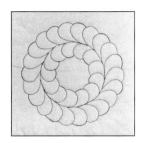

Feathers are one of the most popular free motion machine quilting designs. There are so many different varieties, you may have difficulty choosing one. There are feathered hearts, feathered stars, feathered squares, and feathered wreaths. Feathers are not continuous motion because there is some back tracking involved in the machine quilting.

Quilts with background squares or triangles are especially suited for feathers.

Use this technique with the following Quilt in a Day quilts:

- **Irish Chain**
- **Snowball**
- **Dutch Windmills**

Irish Chain

Feathers

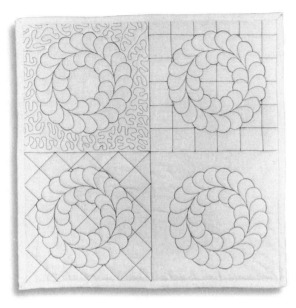

Materials:

one 18" square Heirloom Wool® batting
two 18" squares quilter's muslin
two 3" wide strips for binding
optional pillow form

 Marking pencil

 Darning foot, darning spring, or spring needle

 Feather stencil (provided in back of book)

 Quilt Sew Easy™

 75 one inch Safety pins

 Thread for bobbin

 Kwik Klip™

 Invisible thread

 Cellophane tape

 6" x 24" ruler

Marking One Layer of Muslin

1. Divide one layer of muslin into four quarters by drawing lines at the halfway point both horizontally and vertically.

2. Remove the feather stencil from the back of the book.

3. Center the stencil on each square. With the silver pencil, lightly trace in the lines on the stencil. You should see them without straining your eyes.

4. In the second square, draw the stencil, then draw horizontal and vertical lines spaced 1½" apart.

5. In the third square, draw the stencil, then draw lines diagonally in both directions, spaced 1½" apart.

6. Make the quilt sandwich, pin the layers and close the safety pins.

Setting Up Your Practice

1. Thread the machine with the invisible thread. Loosen the top tension. Thread the bobbin with the regular sewing thread.

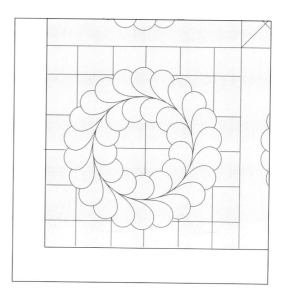

2. Engage your walking foot and secure the layers by sewing on the horizontal and vertical lines.

Setting Up Your Machine for Free Motion Quilting

1. Remove or disengage the walking foot.

2. Put on the darning foot, darning spring, or spring needle.

3. Drop or cover your feed dogs.

Quilting the Sample

Feather Quilting the Muslin Square

With feathers, machine quilt from side to side, catching the vein as you go and backtracking along either the vein or the feather.

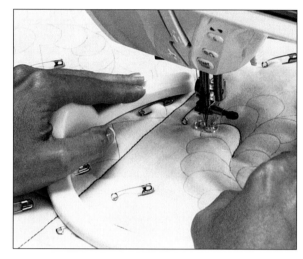

1. Slip the quilt under the darning foot.

2. Place your hands to either side of the motif or use the Quilt Sew Easy™. Check for lumps or folds.

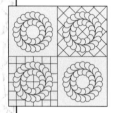

3. Insert the needle at the starting point shown on the stencil. Bring the bobbin thread to the surface. Pull up the slack in the thread. Lock the stitches and continue sewing around the first feather. See numbers 1, 2, and 3 on illustration, page 59.

4. When you reach the point where you meet the next feather, backtrack in the same stitches until you reach the beginning of the next feather. See number 4 on illustration, page 59.

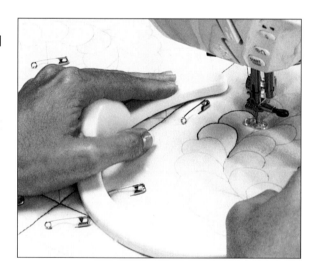

5. Sew around the second feather. When you meet the vein of the feather, follow it back to near where you started. See numbers 5 and 6.

6. Follow a feather on the opposite side. See numbers 7 and 8. When you reach the point where you meet the next feather backtrack in the same stitches until you reach the beginning of the next feather. See number 9.

7. Sew around the fourth feather. See numbers 10, 11, and 12 on illustration. When you meet the vein of the feather, follow it back to near where you last followed the vein. Backtrack in the same stitches until you reach the next feather on the opposite side from where you were just working.

8. Repeat the directions above, alternating from side to side and backtracking where necessary. See 13 and 14.

9. When you reach the point where you started, lock stitches. Bring the bobbin thread up to the top. Clip loose threads.

10. Repeat for remaining feathers in all squares.

Stippling Around the Feather in Square One

1. Slip the quilt under the darning foot.

2. Place your hands to either side of the motif or use the Quilt Sew Easy™. Check for lumps or folds.

3. Insert the needle on the sewing line previously sewn and bring the bobbin thread to the surface. Pull up the slack in the thread. Lock the stitches.

4. Stipple around the motif with your favorite of the three stippling techniques. Be careful not to box yourself into a corner.

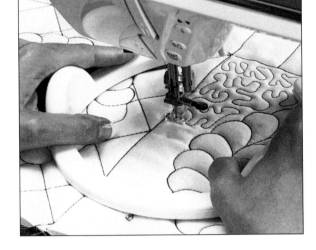

5. When you have filled the area around the motif move toward the edge of either the motif or the securing lines sewn, and lock the stitches. Clip loose threads.

Horizontal and Vertical Quilting in Square Two

1. Remove the darning foot. Raise feed dogs or remove the feed dog cover.

2. Engage your walking foot and set the stitch length to 3 to 4 mm or 8 to 10 stitches per inch.

3. Slip the quilt under the walking foot. Place your hands to either side of the motif or use the Quilt Sew Easy™. Check for lumps or folds.

4. Insert the needle on the horizontal line previously sewn. Bring the bobbin thread to the surface. Pull up the slack in the thread. Lock the stitches.

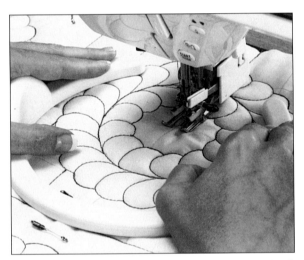

Using Quilt Sew Easy©

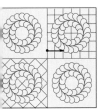

5. Sew along vertical lines drawn until you reach the motif. Lock stitches. Jump across the motif. Lock stitches.

6. Continue to sew vertically. Fill the square around the motif in both directions vertically, locking the stitches and clipping loose threads.

7. Repeat above steps for horizontal lines.

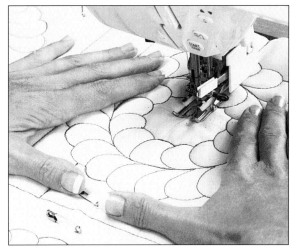

Using hands

Diagonal Grid Quilting Square Three

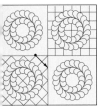

1. Remove the darning foot and engage your walking foot. Set the stitch length to 3 to 4 mm or 8 to 10 stitches per inch.

2. Slip the quilt under the walking foot. Place your hands to either side of the motif or use the Quilt Sew Easy™ as before. Check for lumps.

3. Bring the bobbin thread to the surface. Pull up the slack in the thread. Lock the stitches.

4. Sew along diagonal lines drawn until you reach the motif. Lock stitches. Jump across the motif. Lock stitches.

Using Quilt Sew Easy™

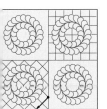

5. Continue to sew diagonally. Fill the square around the motif in both directions diagonally, locking the stitches and clipping loose threads.

Finish the Practice

1. Bind, using the traditional method, page 82 or optional pillow directions, page 62.

2. Remove safety pins and launder.

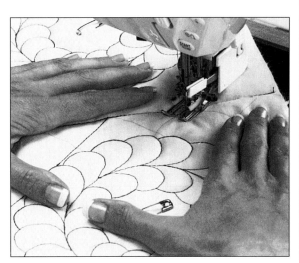

Using hands

Pillow

Materials

one 18" square machine quilted
one 18" pillow form
½ yard fabric for pillow backing
optional fringe or piping

Cut two 12½" x 18" pieces from pillow backing fabric.

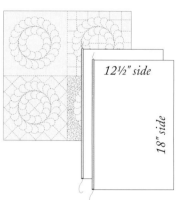

1. Turn under one edge ¼" on each back piece. Press.

2. Turn under the same edge again. Press.

3. Top stitch close to inside folded edge.

4. Add optional trim. Place trim, right sides together, on edge of quilted fabric. Sew in place. At corners, curve trim slightly around corner.

5. Place quilted fabric face up. Place one piece of backing material face down on top of quilted fabric. Place hemmed edges near center of pillow. Pin in place.

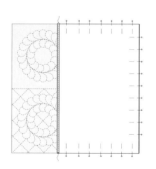

6. Place second piece of backing material face down on remaining side of quilted fabric. Hemmed edges of backing material should overlap. Pin in place.

7. Sew around edge of fabric with a ½" seam.

8. Turn right sides out. Stuff with pillow form.

Stitch in the chain is a good beginner technique that shows up beautifully on this Single Irish Chain by Ruth Griffith. Lines can be marked with a quilter's pencil or Hera marker and quilted using a walking foot. Cynthia Martin also used a feather stencil to add a circular motif in the light background blocks.

Cynthia Martin free motion quilted this motif in the background areas of Sue Bouchard's lovely Tennessee Waltz quilt.

Sue Bouchard's cheerful Christmas quilt, also shown on the cover, was made using the Double Irish Chain and appliqued holly leaves. Cynthia Martin finished the quilt with a variety of machine quilting techniques. Outline quilting defines the holly leaves, while grid quilting enhances the diagonal chains. In the border, Cynthia used a single feather stencil to create a serpentine pattern.

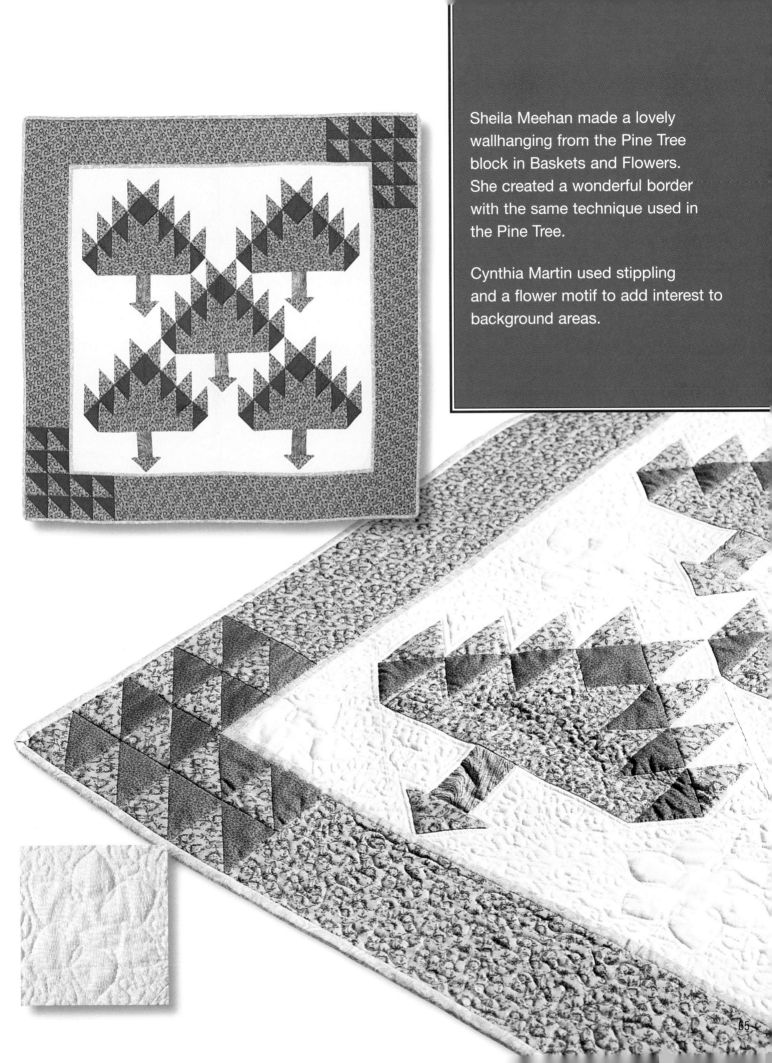

Sheila Meehan made a lovely wallhanging from the Pine Tree block in Baskets and Flowers. She created a wonderful border with the same technique used in the Pine Tree.

Cynthia Martin used stippling and a flower motif to add interest to background areas.

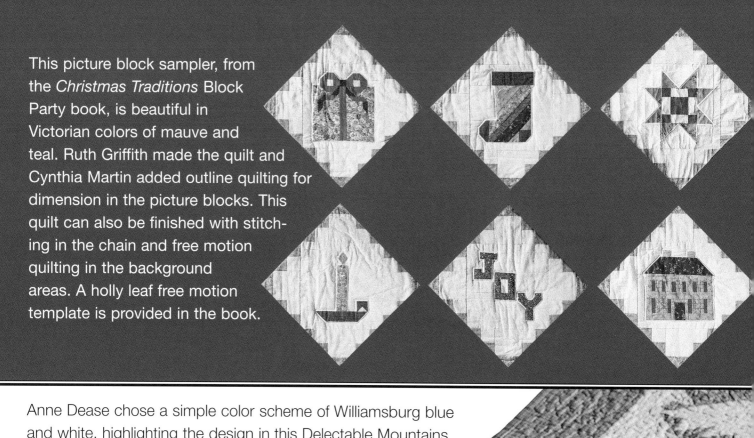

This picture block sampler, from the *Christmas Traditions* Block Party book, is beautiful in Victorian colors of mauve and teal. Ruth Griffith made the quilt and Cynthia Martin added outline quilting for dimension in the picture blocks. This quilt can also be finished with stitching in the chain and free motion quilting in the background areas. A holly leaf free motion template is provided in the book.

Anne Dease chose a simple color scheme of Williamsburg blue and white, highlighting the design in this Delectable Mountains quilt. She used free motion stippling across the entire quilt. After the stippling was completed, she washed and dried her quilt to give it an antique appearance.

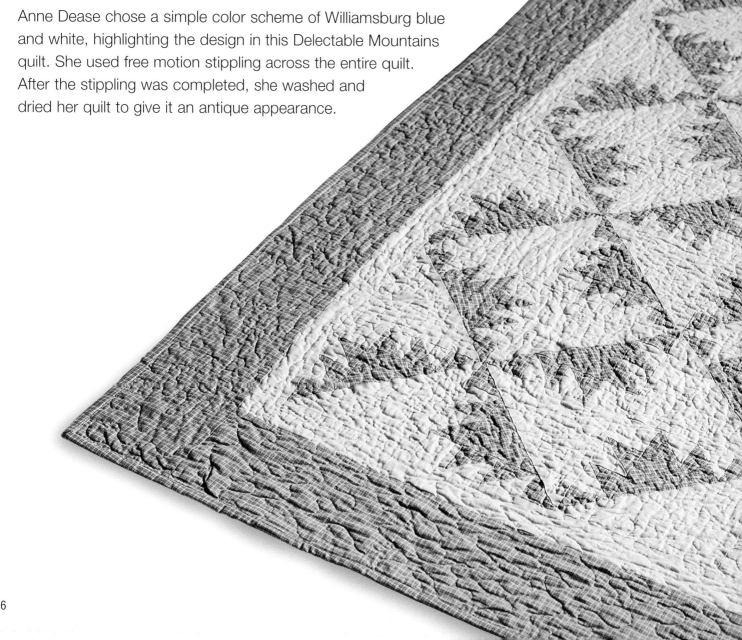

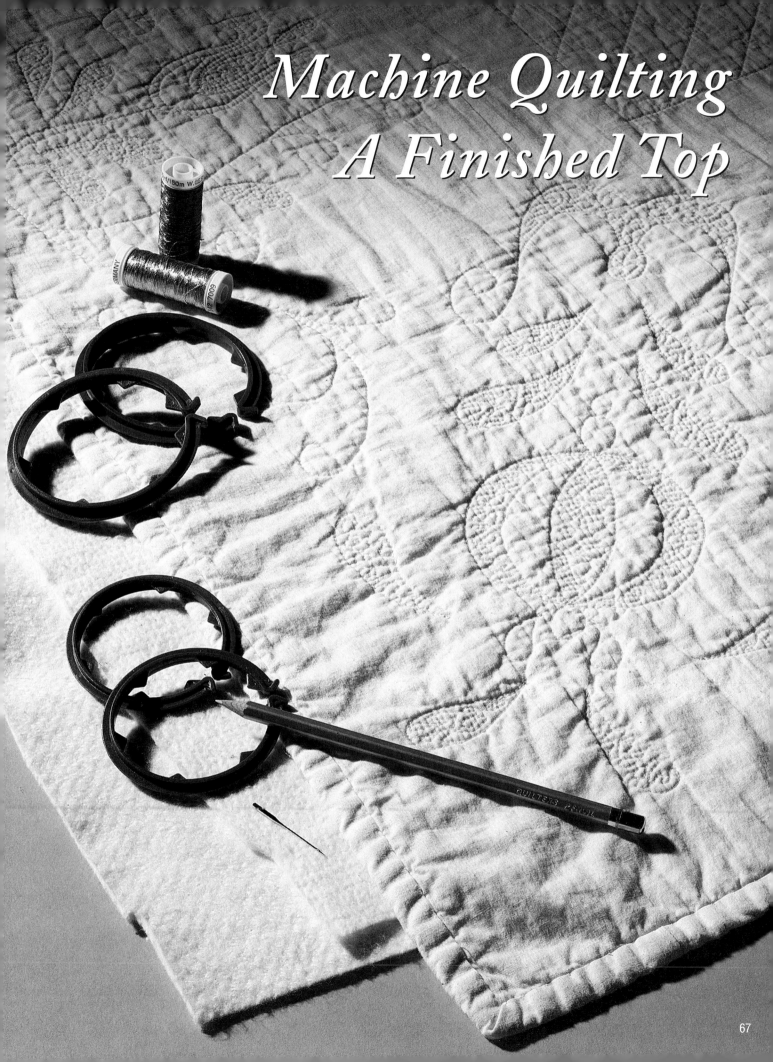

Machine Quilting
A Finished Top

Basics to Get You Started

Markers

There are many types of markers available. Depending on your project, experiment with different types of markers to see which you like best.

Quilter's Pencil

The best tool for marking is the Quilter's Pencil. When the machine quilting is complete and the binding is on the quilt you can either leave the marks or wash the quilt to get rid of them.

Soapstone Marker

Soapstone, a product used in tailoring, is perfect for marking dark fabrics. It is sold under the brand name Treasure Marker® by Cottage Tools. It is similar in shape to a pencil. Lay the quilt stencil on top of the quilt and use the soapstone to draw in the openings of the stencil. Once the quilt top is marked, the marks stay in until removed. Dampen a piece of cloth or paper towel with water and rub over the marked areas or launder the quilt to remove the soapstone marks.

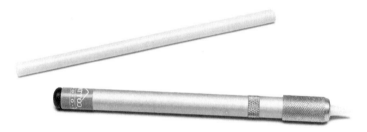

Ultimate Marking Pencil™

The Ultimate Marking Pencil™, or mechanical pencil, is also a good alternative marking tool. It is cushioned so it is comfortable in your hands. Lay the quilt stencil on top of the quilt and use the pencil to draw in the openings of the stencil. The mechanical pencil has a super-fine point which makes a sharp line that is dark enough to see when quilting. The line does not smear and is removed only by laundering.

Fabric Eraser

When using any of the pencil type markers, it may be necessary to use a fabric eraser. This type of eraser is made specifically to be used on fabric and is soft enough that if used properly it should not make fabric balls. It will not smudge the lines and is non-abrasive. If you make a mistake when you are drawing the design on the fabric, erase the line by gently rubbing the area. Don't over-rub as this may cause fabric balls. Then brush the erased area to remove small eraser debris.

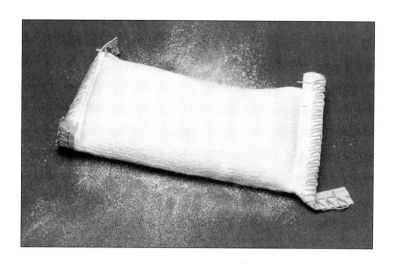

Pouncer

The Pouncer is a chalk-filled bag which comes in two colors, white and blue. Lay the quilt stencil on top of the quilt and touch the openings in the stencil gently with the chalk pouncer. Using the Pouncer is not an assembly-line process. You must pounce only a single area, one block at a time, and quilt it immediately. Otherwise the design will become smudged or disappear before you get a chance to quilt it. The marks can be easily removed by simply brushing them away with your hand.

Chalk

Chalk and chalk products come in a variety of colors. You must chalk only a single area, one block at a time, and quilt it immediately. Otherwise the design will become smudged or disappear before you get a chance to quilt it. The marks can be easily removed by simply brushing them away with your hand. Chalk lines are generally wider than lines drawn with other marking tools, making it hard to follow an intricate design.
White chalk is useful for marking black fabric. Because the lines simply brush away, chalk is useful for marking wallhangings and craft projects you do not intend to launder.

Washout Pens

Washout pens leave marks that are meant to be laundered out. The marks may set in the fabric if it comes in contact with either heat from the sun or from an iron. The directions on some packages imply that simply spraying the fabric with water will remove the mark. Spraying will cause the chemical to move from the top of the quilt into the batting. It is unknown what will happen to the batting if the chemical is left in it for any length of time.

Disappearing Ink Pens

Disappearing ink pens leave marks that are meant to disappear. They are useful for marking craft projects you do not intend to launder. You have 24 hours to quilt the quilt before the ink disappears. It has been my experience that humidity affects the 24 hour number. The higher the humidity, the sooner the marks disappear. The marks could set in the fabric if the fabric comes in contact with either heat from the sun or from an iron. The marks may seem to disappear but the chemical is still on the surface of the quilt top. If the quilt top is not laundered, the marks that are left turn yellow as they age and do not wash out.

Safety Pins

These are the approximate quantities of safety pins needed for various size quilts:

- **Baby size quilt or lap robe**   50-100
- **Twin size quilt**   100-300
- **Double size quilt**   300-400
- **Queen size quilt**   400-600
- **King size quilt**   600-1000

Place safety pins so that they will not interfere with your machine quilting. As a rule of thumb, if you place your hand on an area, you should feel pins under and around your hand. The actual measurement is every 3" to 4" apart. If you are quilting in a straight line, place your pins about ½" to 1" away from the quilting line and every 3" to 4" along the quilting line. Remove any safety pins that are in the way as you sew. Use a Kwik Klip® to close the safety pins.

Safety pins will rust if exposed to moisture. To prevent your pins from rusting, place them in a sealed plastic container such as a large margarine container and place a packet of desiccant in the container as well. Desiccant is a drying agent that absorbs moisture, commonly found in shoe boxes and vitamins. I save all that I find to put in my pin box. You can also purchase desiccant at your local drug store.

Do not leave safety pins in your quilt for an extended length of time. I suggest leaving them in for no more than a month, and in very humid areas even less. Once a rust spot is on the quilt it is nearly impossible to remove. One product on the market that will successfully remove rust every time is *Amazing #2066 Rust and Stain Remover* (GR Enterprises, Escondido, CA). It will remove rust from cotton, linen, silk, and wool without the use of acids if you use it according to the directions.

Decorative Thread

Now that you are experienced, you may want to use something other than invisible or regular sewing machine thread. Use decorative threads as the top quilting thread to add pizzazz to your quilt. Sulky makes great silk-like rayon threads that create beautiful effects. When there are several different colors in different values in your quilt top, try using variegated Sulky thread. Use regular thread to match the backing fabric in the bobbin.

Gold metallic thread looks really special when used on fabric with gold accents. If you are going to sew with metallic thread, you may want to try Schmetz® Microtex Sharp needles which are specifically made for sewing with this type of thread.

Stencils

There are so many different types of stencils that the variety will probably overwhelm you the first time you shop for them. First, look for a design you like, then analyze it for ease of machine quilting. Your first few quilting attempts will be more fun if the stencils are simple. Once you feel comfortable with machine quilting, progress to the more difficult stencils. One suggestion for beginners is to draw in the spaces left out by the stencil. When you are machine quilting, you cannot always see the complete design. Drawing in the connecting lines makes the machine quilting easier and less stressful.

What if I Can't See the Line I Drew?

If the line is too light to see, you will need to darken it. If it is behind the foot, move your head so you can see the line. Judge the direction of the line. Continue to sew. I call this "guesstimation". Remember that when you are all done quilting, you will launder the quilt and the lines will be gone.

Making Your Own Stencils

You may find that a stencil you like is too large or small for the area you want to quilt. You can enlarge or reduce its size by photocopying the stencil and then making your own with template mylar. If you like, you can make an original stencil from your own design.

1. Doodle on paper until you come up with something you like.

2. Lay the design on a work surface (not your dining table top) and secure it to the surface with tape.

3. Lay the template mylar on top of the design and secure it with tape.

4. Use either an Exacto® blade or a mylar template burning tool to create the open spaces in the stencil. Make sure that when you are cutting, you leave connected areas, otherwise the stencil will literally fall apart.

Parts of the Quilt

Batting

There are many brands of polyester, cotton, and wool batting on the market. The type of batting you choose will depend on your project and the effect you wish to achieve. Whatever the batting type, it is important to pay attention to the batting weight.

Batting Weight

Bonded polyester battings come in several weights. For machine quilting, do not use batting thicker than 12 oz weight. When you are machine quilting, you must be concerned with how much batting will fit in the neck of the sewing machine. Batting that is more than 12 oz will be very difficult to work with.

Rolled battings come in specific ounces and widths, and can be deceptive. Batting weight is determined by how much it weighs per yard. For example, a 6 oz, 96" wide piece of batting off the roll is actually the same thickness as a 3 oz, 48" wide piece. It has just been doubled and folded over. Bagged batting generally uses terms such as low loft, medium loft, and high loft, which are hard to define without seeing and feeling the batting.

Bagged Batting versus Batting on the Roll

I recommend purchasing batting off the roll instead of in the bag if possible. Bagged batting is tightly folded and tends to retain the folds until the batting relaxes. To get it to relax, you must either lay the batting out on a flat surface overnight or put it into the dryer and tumble with no heat. Most stores don't like you to open a batting bag because it is hard to resell. If you want to feel the batting, ask before opening it.

Batting off the roll has only one fold down the middle. That fold relaxes fairly quickly so the batting can be put directly in the quilt. You can also see and feel the weight before purchasing it.

Batting Comparison Chart

Brand	Manufacturer	Style & Fiber	Quilt Distance	Loft
Polydown (Black)	Hobbs	Polyester Bonded	4" - 6"	¼" - ⅜"
Polyester	Hobbs	Polyester Bonded	4" - 6"	¼" - ⅜"
Warm and Natural	Warm Products	100% cotton Needle punched	10"	⅛"
Heirloom Cotton	Hobbs	80% cotton 20% polyester Bonded	3"	⅛" - 3⁄16"
Wool Naturally	Warm Products	100% wool Needle punched	10"	¼"
Heirloom 100% Wool	Hobbs	100% wool Bonded	3"	¼" - ⅜"

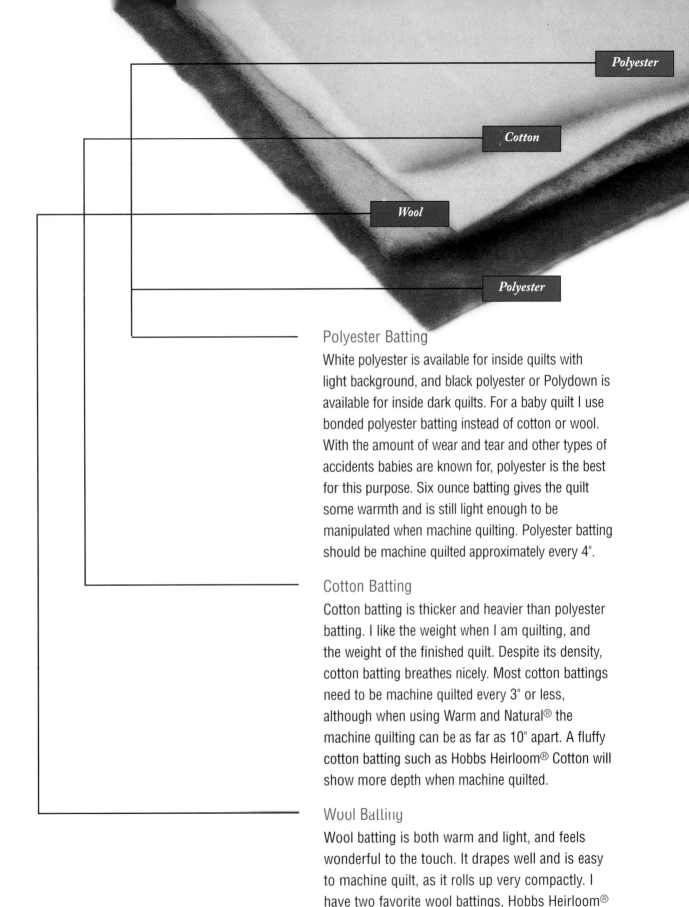

Polyester Batting

White polyester is available for inside quilts with light background, and black polyester or Polydown is available for inside dark quilts. For a baby quilt I use bonded polyester batting instead of cotton or wool. With the amount of wear and tear and other types of accidents babies are known for, polyester is the best for this purpose. Six ounce batting gives the quilt some warmth and is still light enough to be manipulated when machine quilting. Polyester batting should be machine quilted approximately every 4".

Cotton Batting

Cotton batting is thicker and heavier than polyester batting. I like the weight when I am quilting, and the weight of the finished quilt. Despite its density, cotton batting breathes nicely. Most cotton battings need to be machine quilted every 3" or less, although when using Warm and Natural® the machine quilting can be as far as 10" apart. A fluffy cotton batting such as Hobbs Heirloom® Cotton will show more depth when machine quilted.

Wool Batting

Wool batting is both warm and light, and feels wonderful to the touch. It drapes well and is easy to machine quilt, as it rolls up very compactly. I have two favorite wool battings, Hobbs Heirloom® and Wool Naturally® by Warm Products. You can machine quilt Heirloom® washable wool batting up to 3" apart, and Wool Naturally™ up to 10" apart.

Backing

The back of the quilt is just as important as the front. The backing fabric can be muslin, a print fabric, a solid colored fabric, a fabric used in the top, or scraps of all the top fabrics. Whatever you choose to use, the backing fabric needs to be the same quality as the fabric used in the top. A sheet or a poor quality backing fabric will not have the same thread count as the quilt fabrics. When laundering a quilt made with fabrics of different quality, uneven shrinkage may occur. This will prevent the quilt from lying flat, or cause lumpiness.

I suggest that the fabric be all of one piece if possible. White and muslin fabrics for backing are made up to 120" wide, while some print fabrics can be found up to 90" wide. This alleviates the need to piece the backing. Purchase backing fabric that is at least 4" wider and longer that the quilt top. For example, if the top measures 86" x 92", purchase 2⅝ yards of 96" wide fabric.

Piecing the Back

Your top may be so large that the backing fabric must be pieced. You may wish to piece a backing from fabrics used in the top. Remove the selvage edges and sew a lengthwise seam to piece the backing together. Press seams open. A lengthwise seam will be less of a point of stress. If possible, utilizing a horizontal seam uses less yardage.

Fabric widths vary from 40" to 45" wide. To determine how much backing fabric you need, measure the quilt top and then measure the width of the backing fabric.

These examples are based on 40" wide fabric. If your fabric is 45" wide, you may need less fabric.

If your quilt top is 36" wide or less you need one length of 40" fabric plus an additional 4".

If your quilt top is under 76" wide, and your backing fabric is 40" wide, add 4" to the length and purchase twice that length.

If your quilt top is more than 76" wide, add 4" to the length and purchase three times that length.

This is an example for a 76" x 96" quilt top:

96" + 4" = 100"	Length Plus 4"
100" x 2 = 200"	Multiplied by 2
200" ÷ 36 = 5.5 yds	Divided by 36" (1 yd)
	Round up to 5¾ yds

Backing Color

In deciding what color of backing to use, first plan where you will be quilting on the front. In general, the bobbin thread color is matched to the backing fabric. It is best to use the same color of thread on the top and on the bobbin, because you sometimes see a trace of thread from the opposite side. For instance, if you are quilting the light background on the top, use muslin or white fabric on the back and cream or white thread on top and in the bobbin. When quilting an Amish quilt, use black fabric on the back and black thread. You may also wish to use black batting. If you use a backing print which has several shades of a particular color and the upper thread is invisible thread, try a variegated thread in the bobbin that matches the backing fabric.

Preparing the Top for Quilting

Now it's time for you to practice on the real thing. I suggest that your first real quilt be a small one such as a baby quilt. A word of caution, baby quilts should not be quilted with invisible thread. If the stitching becomes loose, it can damage little fingers. When you feel comfortable, move on to the larger sized quilts. The following describes in detail the sequence of layering the quilt and securing the layers.

Pressing

Press your quilt top prior to marking. Press from the wrong side first, pressing the seams in the same direction as they were stitched. Press from the right side, making certain there are no tucks or folds.

Marking the Single Layer

If you need to mark lines or trace stencils, mark the quilt top as a single layer. Your markings tend to widen if you mark the quilt after layering. Make sure your marks are not too dark or too light. You should be able to see the marks clearly in regular light. If you use a Hera Marker, it is better to mark in stages after the quilt top is layered.

Layering the Quilt

Layout Table

A common question is what to use to lay out a quilt if your floor and dining table are too small. A ping pong table is perfect.

In the Quilt in a Day classroom we use three sawhorses with two sheets of 4' x 8' particle board over them. We seal the particle board with a varnish. Sawhorse tables are inexpensive and they can be stored against a wall when not in use. The key to making the table is cutting the sawhorse legs at a comfortable pinning/layout height. Because everyone is proportioned differently, that number will be individual to you. As a rule of thumb, a table set at approximately your waist height should be comfortable for you. A single sheet of 4' x 8' particle board is large enough for any small quilt up to twin size. Two sheets of 4' x 8' particle board are large enough for double and queen size but a king will hang over the edge. This is acceptable. When you finish pinning the areas of the king size quilt on the table, simply move the pinned area off and the unpinned area onto the table. Then complete the pinning.

Backing

Place your backing face down on your layout table and secure it with tape or large 3" binder clamps. Binder clamps are available from any office supply store. Smooth out the backing, then clamp two opposite sides. Then clamp the remaining sides. Do not stretch the backing. Smooth it out and secure it without stretching or pulling. Make sure your backing is at least 2" larger than the top on all four sides.

Batting

Next, place your batting of choice on top of the backing without clamping or taping. Smooth the batting but do not stretch or pull it out of shape. Again, make sure your batting is at least 2" larger than the top. If you use packaged batting, it is a good idea to let it rest and "breathe" for twenty-four hours so the folds fall out. You can also put it in the dryer on the fluff cycle.

Quilt Top

Last, place the pre-marked quilt top face up on top of the batting and smooth it. Make sure that the quilt remains square by placing a 16" Square-up ruler in each corner. Adjust the quilt if it is not square by smoothing the top toward or away from the area that is not square. Check to see that the borders are smoothed straight.

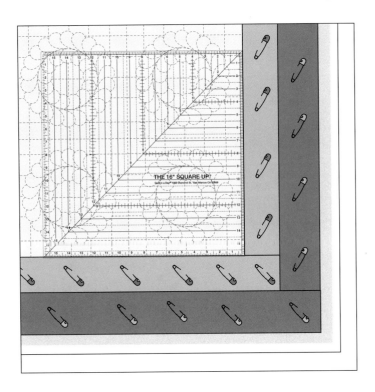

Pinning

After you layer the quilt, it is ready for pinning. Safety pin through all layers. As you pin you should feel the surface of the table or floor. If you do not pin all the way through, the layers could shift. Pin from the center of the quilt out. Make sure you pin enough to secure the layers. A good rule of thumb is one pin for every 3".

Instead of using safety pins, layers can be held together with a thin plastic tack.

Basting Tacker

The basting tacker has a specially designed needle that shoots a thin plastic tack into the quilt layers to hold them. A plastic grid is placed under the quilt layers which lifts the layers up and allows the needle to be inserted. The grid is moved under the layers as you baste the quilt. Use the same amount of basting tacks as for the safety pin basting method. The basting tacker has several advantages, including speed and being lighter in weight than pins. Once the quilting process is complete, tacks are removed by cutting them apart with scissors. The plastic tacks will not rust over time or break your sewing machine needle if you sew over them. However, the tacks are not re-usable. The needle in the basting tacker should be replaced frequently. If it becomes dull, it will break threads in the fabric as it is inserted through the layers. The plastic grid can be hard to move under the layers of the quilt.

Adjustment of Tension

Check your sewing machine tension on scraps of batting between two layers of scrap backing. The stitches must lock in the middle of the batting and not on the top or the bottom. When using invisible thread, lower the upper tension. If the tension does not look balanced before you quilt, it will not look balanced after you quilt.

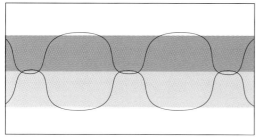

Good stitches lock inside the layers.

Getting perfect tension can sometimes be difficult. Use the following examples to help you determine whether your tension is correct or needs adjustment. When your sewing machine's tension is balanced, the bobbin thread and upper thread tie off in the center of the fabric. With balanced tension you do not see the bobbin thread on the top of the quilt or the upper thread on the back of the quilt.

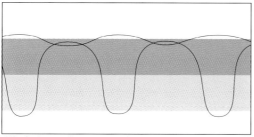

If stitches pull to top surface, reduce upper tension.

If the bobbin thread is peeking through and showing on the top, the upper tension is too tight. To balance the tension, lower the upper tension. Reduce the upper tension number to a smaller number in a small increment. (If the tension was 4.5, reduce the upper tension to 4.) Always check the tension by machine quilting a small area. If the adjustment fixes the problem, proceed with the machine quilting, otherwise lower the tension further and retest.

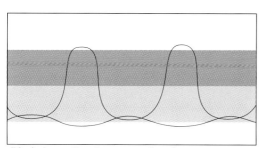

If stitches pull to bottom surface, increase upper tension.

If the upper thread is peeking through and showing on the bottom, this means that the upper tension is too loose. To balance the tension, you need to tighten the upper tension. Increase the upper tension number to a larger number. (If the tension was 4.5 increase the upper tension to 5 and machine quilt to check the tension.) If the adjustment fixes the problem, proceed with the machine quilting, otherwise, raise the tension further and retest.

Clips

Quilt clips are designed to hold a rolled quilt and to control the bulk of the quilt during the machine quilting process. Two of my favorites are Jaws™ and Quilt Clips™. Jaws™ have teeth so they slide less on the quilt. Quilt Clips™ are flat on one side so they roll less. By turning the clip so the flat side is up, the clip can be slipped over the top edge of the table surface, securing the quilt layers. It's a substitute for binder clamps when layering the quilt.

Rolling

Roll the quilt when you are ready to begin machine quilting. This makes it easier to insert through the throat of the sewing machine. Roll the quilt as tightly as possible from both sides toward the middle of the quilt. Use clips to hold the roll neatly.

Managing a Large Quilt

Insert the area to sew under the needle with one roll under the neck of the machine and the other roll to the left.

The rest of the quilt can be placed over your shoulder with a loop of the quilt in your lap. It can also be folded accordion style and placed on your lap so that the layer on top is the first to be sewn.

After you finish a section, unroll the clipped layers that are under the neck of the machine and roll the quilted section into the clipped layers to the left.

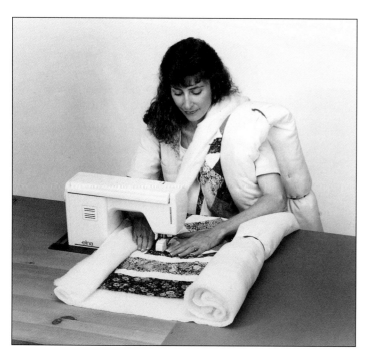

Starting to Quilt
Quilting Order

The first areas to be machine quilted will help to stabilize the quilt. Most quilts have either horizontal and vertical or diagonal block placement. Machine quilt either horizontally and vertically or diagonally first. Start with the longest line of machine quilting, such as corner to corner on a diagonal quilt. Then machine quilt the other diagonal corner to corner. This leaves only four unstabilized areas. Machine quilt the remaining diagonals as you unroll the quilt. The first few rows in the middle will be the most difficult. Once you stabilize the quilt, then move on to the individual blocks themselves, using your favorite machine quilting method. The last sections to be quilted are the borders. This way, any excess fabric will move out to the border where it will not show as you machine quilt.

You need to heavily quilt the borders if the blocks are heavily quilted.

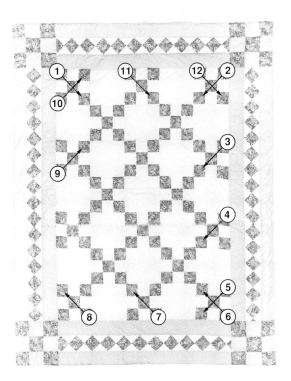

Begin Sewing

Begin sewing by pulling the bobbin thread to the top. If you do not pull the bobbin thread to the top, you will sew it into your machine quilting which results in a terrible mess on the back side of the quilt. To do this, take a single stitch, then pull on the upper thread. You will then see a small loop appear which is the bobbin thread.

Once the bobbin thread is on the surface, begin stitching by inserting the needle in the same hole as you previously made. If you are using the walking foot, lock your stitch by sewing back and forth several times and clip the threads. If you are using the darning foot, lock the stitch by moving the quilt and stitching back and forth at least three times. Clip the threads. When you are at the end of the design, lock off your stitches. Then bring the bobbin thread to the top by pulling on the upper thread. Clip the threads. This eliminates having to lift the quilt and clip the threads from the back.

What if My Thread Breaks or Runs Out as I am Sewing?

If your thread breaks, cut the remaining thread so your project is loose. Pull up the stitches to the top with the stiletto and trim them flush with the top. About ¼" from the break, along the previously sewn line, insert your needle, pull up the bobbin thread, lock stitches, and then continue to sew.

Changing Needles

When I ask my students how often they change their sewing machine needle the typical answer is, "When it breaks." They do not realize that the needle was probably dull long before it broke and could have been breaking the threads in the fabric. Change your sewing machine needle after every eight hours of continuous sewing. You may need to change your needle four or more times on a king size quilt depending upon the amount of machine quilting involved. If you do not change the needle, it may cause thread breakage in the fabric or the thread itself may break as you are machine quilting.

Finishing Your Quilt

Binding - Two Methods - Traditional and Reverse Traditional

How to figure binding

Strip Size	Finished Size
3" strips	⅝" wide finished binding
2½" strips	½" wide finished binding
2" strips	⅜" wide finished binding

Example for a quilt measuring 90" x 96".

90" + 96" = 186"   Measure the width and length of the quilt. Add the two numbers together.

186" x 2 = 372"   Multiply this number by two.

372" + 12" = 384"   Add 12" to that number for mitering corners.

384" ÷ 40 = 8.5   Divide this number by 40", or the width of your fabric from selvage to selvage. This is the number of strips you need to cut.

9   Round up to a full strip.

3"   Next determine how wide you want your binding.

9 x 3" = 27"   Multiply the number of strips needed by the width of the strips to find the yardage needed.
or ⅞ yd

Preparing the Binding

1. Square off the selvage edges, and sew binding pieces together into one long strip.

2. Press the binding strip in half lengthwise with right sides out.

3. Place a walking foot attachment and regular thread on top and in the bobbin to match the binding. Use 10 stitches per inch, or #3 setting.

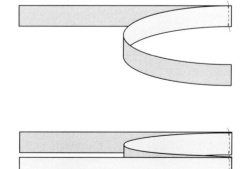

Traditional Binding

The binding is wrapped from the front of the quilt to the back.

1. Line up the raw edges of the folded binding with the raw edge on the right side of the quilt at the middle of one side.

2. Begin sewing 4" from the end of the binding.

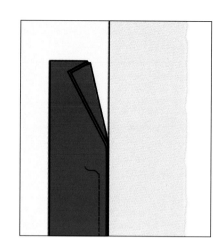

3. At the corner, stop the stitching ¼" from the edge with the needle in the fabric. Raise the presser foot and turn the quilt to the next side. Put the foot back down.

4. Sew backwards ¼" to the edge of the binding, raise the foot, and pull the quilt forward slightly.

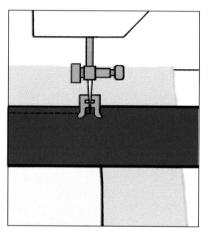

5. Fold the binding strip straight up on the diagonal. Fingerpress in the diagonal fold.

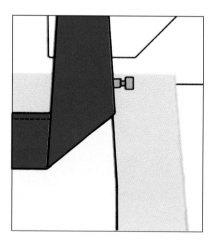

6. Fold the binding strip straight down with the diagonal fold underneath. Line up the top of the fold with the raw edge of the binding underneath.

7. Begin sewing from the corner.

8. Continue sewing and mitering the corners around the outside of the quilt.

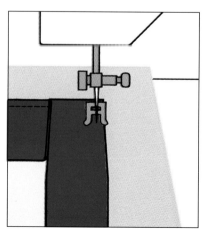

9. Stop sewing 4" from where the ends will overlap.

10. Line up the two ends of binding. Trim the excess with a ½" overlap.

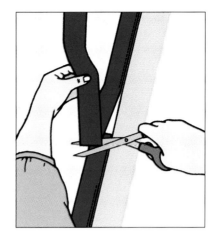

11. Open out the folded ends and pin right sides together. Sew a ¼" seam.

12. Continue to sew the binding in place.

13. Trim the batting and backing up to the raw edges of the binding.

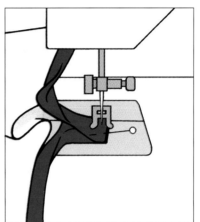

14. For handstitched finish, see page 86. For machine finish, pin in place so that the folded edge on the binding covers the stitching line. Tuck in the excess fabric on the diagonal at each miter.

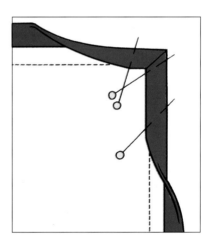

15. From the right side, "stitch in the ditch" using invisible thread on the right side, and a bobbin thread to match the binding on the back side. Catch the folded edge of the binding on the back side with the stitching.

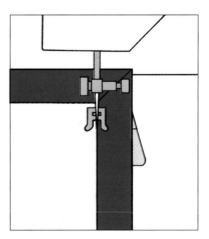

Cynthia's Reverse Traditional Binding Method

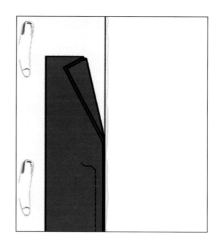

The binding is wrapped from the back of the quilt to the front.

1. Using safety pins, pin 1" to 2" away from the edge of the quilt top, making sure the layers are all smoothed to the outside and flat. Trim away excess batting and backing flush with the quilt top.

2. Line up the raw edge of the folded binding with the raw edge of the backing at the middle of the right side of the quilt.

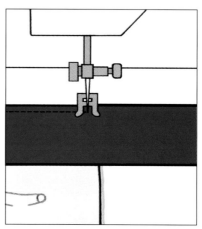

3. Begin sewing 4" from the end of the binding.

4. At the corner, stop the stitching ¼" from the edge with the needle in the fabric. Raise the presser foot and turn the quilt to the next side. Put the foot back down.

5. Sew backwards ¼" to the edge of the binding, raise the foot, and pull the quilt forward slightly.

6. Fold the binding strip straight up on the diagonal. Fingerpress in the diagonal fold.

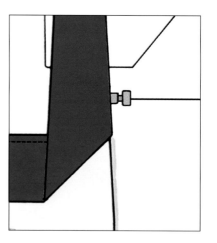

7. Fold the binding strip straight down with the diagonal fold underneath. Line up the top of the fold with the raw edge of the binding underneath.

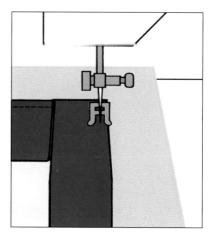

8. Begin sewing from the corner.

9. Continue sewing and mitering the corners around the outside of the quilt.

10. Stop sewing 4" from where the ends will overlap.

11. Line up the two ends of binding. Trim the excess with a ½" overlap.

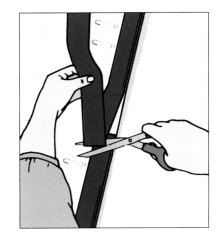

12. Open out the folded ends and pin right sides together. Sew a ¼" seam.

13. Continue to sew the binding in place.

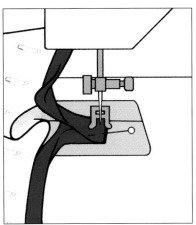

14. For a hand stitched finish see page 86. For a machine finish, fold the binding to the front side of the quilt. Pin in place so that the folded edge on the binding covers the stitching line. Tuck in the excess fabric on the diagonal at each miter.

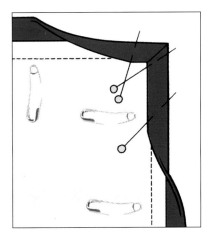

15. From the right side, use a zigzag, blind hem stitch, or decorative stitch to sew the binding to the front. Use invisible thread on the top, and a bobbin thread to match the backing. Catch the folded edge of the binding on the top side with the stitching.

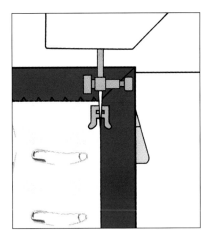

Hand Stitch Finish
Binding Clips

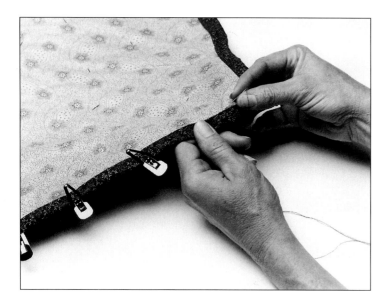

Binding clips are made of rust-proof nickel plated steel and are approximately 2" long. They are excellent for firmly holding the binding as you hand sew. They will not fall out of the binding or stick you as quilter's straight pins. They are fast and easy to place along the binding edge. First, fold the binding over to cover the stitch line. Place binding clips about 3" apart along the edge of the binding. Hand stitch the binding down.

Labeling

Once the binding is on your quilt, complete it with a label. On the label, put your name, the date it was completed, and perhaps a dedication to the person you are giving it to. Labels give the quilt the finishing touch and help others to document quilts in the future. You wouldn't believe the number of beautiful quilts that are unidentified because quiltmakers failed to label them.

A Pigma pen or permanent ink pen can be used to hand sign your quilt label. Heat set ink with an iron before sewing label to quilt. You could also stitch letters or a saying with computerized sewing machine.

Another nice way of finishing is to hand sew on a designer label signed with a permanent ink Pigma pen.

Quilt labels designed by Susan McKelvey

Index

Quilt in a Day®

For successful machine quilting, it is important to have the correct tools. The following supplies can be ordered from Quilt in a Day:

Invisible thread
Hera Marker
Schmetz® needles
Quilter's Pencil
Quilt Clips™
Quilt Sew Easy™
Jaws™ clips
Kwik Klip™
Stiletto
Curved or straight safety pins
Rotary cutter
Cutting mat
Quilter's straight pins
Quilter's soap
6" X 24" ruler
Stencils
Quilter's tape
Darning Spring
Ultimate Marking Pencil™
Treasure Marker®
Quilt in a Day labels

You can purchase these products from the following listed suppliers:

Sew Steady Table Extenders:
Dream World Enterprises
P.O. Box 192
Bonners Ferry ID 83805
(208)267-7136

Parsons Table Inserts:
Brewer Sewing Supplies
3800 West 42nd Street
Chicago IL 60632
(800)444-3111

Amazing #2066 Rust and Stain Remover:
GR Enterprises
2316 Vineyard Avenue
Escondido CA 92029
(619)480-4484

Contact your local sewing machine dealer to order a darning foot, walking foot, or quilter's guide for your machine.

Quilt in a Day® • 1955 Diamond Street • San Marcos, CA 92078
www.quiltinaday.com • E-Mail: qiad@quiltinaday.com
760 591-0929 • 800 777-4852 • FAX 760 591-4424